STUDIES FOR

MW00674145

SLAYING THE DRAGON

of

EVOLUTION

Isaac V. Manly, M.D.

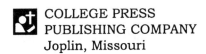

COLLEGE PRESS
PUBLISHING COMPANY
Joplin, Missouri

International Standard Book Number 0-89900-831-3

CONTENTS

Special Studies

STUDIES FOR SMALL GROUPS

Welcome to the *Studies for Small Groups* series from College Press. This series is designed for simplicity of use while giving insight into important issues of the Christian life. Some, like the present volume, will be topical studies. Others will examine a passage of Scripture for the day-to-day lessons we can learn from it.

A number of possible uses could be made of this study. Because there are a limited number of lessons, the format is ideal for new or potential Christians who can begin the study without feeling that they are tied into an overly long commitment. It could also be used for one or two months of weekly studies by a home Bible study group. The series is suitable for individual as well as group study.

Of course, any study is only as good as the effort you put into it. The group leader should study each lesson carefully before the group study session, and if possible, come up with additional Scriptures and other supporting material. Although study questions are provided for each lesson, it would also be helpful if the leader can add his or her own questions.

Neither is it necessary to complete a full lesson in one class period. If the discussion is going well, don't feel that you have to cut it off to fit time constraints, as long as the discussion is related to the topic and not off on side issues.

College Press is happy to present this new 12-lesson study in the *Studies for Small Groups* series, *Slaying the Dragon of Evolution*, based on Ike Manly's earlier work, *God Made*, published by College Press in 1994.

Because of the complexity of this subject, it is impossible to cover all the issues that come up in relation to it or to discuss the evidences as thoroughly as in a longer book. For this reason, we strongly recommend that the discussion leader should consult other sources. Some suggestions are included at the back of this study book, on pp. 83,84.

SLAYING THE DRAGON OF EVOLUTION

We are told in Revelation 4:11: "Thou art worthy, O Lord, to receive glory and honour and power; for thou hast created all things, and for thy pleasure they are and were created."

We recognize God's authority, glory, honor, and His very being through His creation. Yet our public schools and most universities are teaching our children that a man named Darwin came up with what amounts to a way to dodge God's authority.

Many, or perhaps most of us do not buy evolution, but we also do not pay the theory enough attention to learn whether it really has any validity. We also do not know the true facts to teach our children. It is our belief against the belief of others.

I became a Christian at an early age, having been blessed with Christian parents. In medical school I was taught evolution as fact, like most youngsters are taught now. My professors were wonderful people whom I respected tremendously. However, they had been taught evolution as fact also, and my textbooks all presented evolutionary biology as fact. I had enough faith to believe God had created the universe, the earth, and life. It seemed reasonable to think He used evolution to do the job of gradually evolving "simple life" into complex life. I now know there is no such thing as "simple life." Like many of us I became a so-called "theistic evolutionist."

Many of us take this route, and we really do not see too much wrong with it, largely because we do not study Scripture enough to see the confusion resulting in our doctrine. Furthermore, the evolutionary doctrine insists that the universe and all of life came to be by pure chance. It insists that the hydrogen atoms of the Big Bang evolved into man, and that humans are no better than slime.

When I assumed a teaching role in Bible study, I discovered that the theory of evolution really led to confusion about Bible doctrine, and varying amounts of disbelief in God's word, especially the book of Genesis. I was initially intrigued by what I recognized as some similarity between the sequence account of creation in Genesis, and the sequences claimed by evolutionists. I set out to reassure Christians that they could amalgamate the two versions. I delved into biological science, and I was shocked. I found myself reliving the story I read as a youth by Hans Christian Anderson about *The Emperor's New Clothes*,[1] how everybody except a simple boy was afraid to proclaim the truth about the emperor's nakedness.

The most convincing evidence taught to me in medical school was the claim that human embryos go through stages of recapitulation, a claim by evolutionists that embryonic development retraces stages in supposed evolutionary history. We all memorized the catchy phrase "ontogeny recapitulates phylogeny," promulgated by a German enthusiast for Darwinism, Ernst Haeckel, professor of zoology at Jena, Germany. He had falsified drawings of human embryos to make them appear indistinguishable from the embryos of other vertebrates, progressing through a series of stages including "gill slits" in the neck region like fish, and a tail like a monkey. This fraud was recognized and publicized by Professor Wilhelm His, Sr., a prominent embryologist at the University of Leipzig. Haeckel was disgraced, and yet this fraudulent concept was taught to me 69 years after it was disproved, and it is still being taught in many private and public schools, colleges, and universities.

In today's moral climate it is absolutely vital that we not simply have our "belief" against their "belief." As Peter wrote in I Peter 3:15, "But sanctify the Lord God in your hearts, and be ready always to give an answer to every man that asketh you a reason of the hope that is in you with meekness and fear."

Many of our doctrines come from Genesis 1 and 2, and they are extolled in the words of the prophets, and in our hymns of praise. From them we learn that we are made in the image of God with the ability to communicate with Him, and to do His will for our lives; that we are expected to be stewards of His creation; that marriage is sacred; and He tells us ten times in chapter one that He created living things after their kinds, meaning that dogs come from dogs, and cats come from cats, and horses come from horses, and monkeys from monkeys. I believe He was warning us that somebody was going to try to tell us someday that horses come from Eohippus, that men come from monkeys, and that everything in the universe comes from the hydrogen atoms let loose by the "Big Bang," wherever that came from.

---

[1] Hans Christian Anderson, 1805-1875.

9

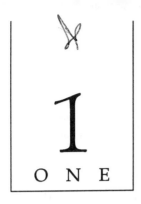

1
O N E

ORIGIN OF SPECIES – HOW SCIENTIFIC?

"Then the Lord answered Job out of the whirlwind, and said, who is this that darkeneth counsel by words without knowledge? Gird up now thy loins like a man; for I will demand of thee, and answer thou me. Where wast thou when I laid the foundations of the earth? Declare if thou hast understanding." Job 38:1-4.

Charles Darwin elected to enter Cambridge University to study for the ministry as an "acceptable" profession. Upon graduation he chose not to be ordained. Although he had no degree in science, he was hired to perform geological surveys for Professors Adam Sedgwick and John Stevens Henslow who had befriended him. It was Henslow who recommended him to sail as a naturalist on the British HMS Beagle on the famous voyage to Tierra del Fuego, South Seas, Indian Archipelago, and back to England. It was this voyage which nourished his concepts of origins.

Darwin had already been exposed to a theory of naturalistic origins by his grandfather, Erasmus Darwin, a noted physician and naturalist, who had written a book entitled *Zoonomia*. Further, very significant influence was provided by Charles Lyell, whose *Principles of Geology* was read while on the voyage. This book convinced Darwin that, contrary to popular opinion of the day, the earth was the result of slow, gradual changes due to processes such as wind, water, and frost. Lyell's theories at that time were radical, but for Darwin they were to satisfy the immense amount of time needed for his theories. It has turned out that the combined theories of Lyell and Darwin have influenced geologists and biologists ever since.

After leaving the South American shores the Beagle sailed to the Galapagos Archipelago, the "Islands of the Tortoises." Giant land tortoises, swimming lizards, and several varieties of finches intrigued Darwin.

NATURAL SELECTION

The variations of animals on Galapagos also fascinated Darwin. There were many finches and these were quite variable. The seed eaters had large, heavy beaks like cardinals, and the insect eaters had small, sharp beaks. Darwin supposed these islands had been isolated for millions of years, and the seeds were being planted in his head that gradual change could explain the change of one kind of organism to another. This reasoning is called extrapolation, of which true scientists are taught to be very wary. What Darwin was seeing was variation within kinds, which is what God created when He created sexual reproduction, providing the intermixing of genes. This concept allows organisms to adjust within limits to changes of environment. Evolutionists continue until this day to confuse this gift, which they call "microevolution." It is not change of one basic kind to another — it is variation by the mixing of genes. The finches of Galapagos remained finches, and the tortoises remained tortoises, just as some of us have blue eyes, and some brown eyes, and some have dark skin, and some have light skin, etc.

The variations of animals on Galapagos fascinated Darwin.

DEVELOPING THEORY

After his return to England Darwin continued to observe variations among various plants and animals. He was particularly interested in the many and striking differences in domesticated pigeons.

We must realize that Darwin was not privy to the vast amount of scientific, biological knowledge which has accumulated since his time. Gregor Mendel, an Austrian monk experimenting with inheritance patterns of garden plants, developed the idea of particulate inheritance. We now recognize these elements as genes. He published his findings and theories in 1866, but *there is no evidence that Darwin was aware of Mendel's contributions.*

> There is no evidence that Darwin was aware of Mendel's contributions.

This gap in scientific knowledge, though, was no hindrance to the seeds of evolution that Darwin planted in the fertile ground of his day. Those seeds were to grow into the pseudo-science that undergirds evolutionary theory of today. Darwin picked up one very illusory "philosophy" which continues to distort the understanding of many evolutionists who should know better — i.e., the concept of "inheritance of acquired characters," or "Lamarckism." Jean Baptiste de Lamarck postulated this theory that need, use, and disuse, with inheritance of acquired characteristics, influenced evolution. Through modern science we now know that DNA, the blueprint of life, is not altered by these factors, and even mutations fail to produce new organs — see Chapter 9.

Darwin was encouraged to publish his theories about natural selection and speciation, but he delayed until he received a manuscript from Alfred Russel Wallace. In this manuscript Wallace explained the principle of natural selection of improved types, which was paramount to Darwin's theory. Darwin and Wallace together presented this concept to the Linnaean Society of London in July 1858, and Darwin published *The Origin of Species* in 1859.

This book was enthusiastically received by some, and others were shocked. Atheists then, as now, saw their opportunity to escape ever having to face God. The clergy were grieved, but like many today, made up their own accommodation of Scripture.

ORIGIN OF SPECIES REVISITED

When one reads *On the Origin of Species by Means of Natural Selection* today, *one is struck by the lack of any scientific data, and Darwin's arguments are pure conjecture.* A typical example: "In these chapters I have endeavored to show that if we make due allowance for our ignorance —, if we remember how ignorant we are with respect to the many curious means of occasional transport, — the difficulty is not insuperable in believing that all individuals of the same species, wherever found, are descended from common parents."[1]

There was a tendency then, as well as now, for some to accept any explanation for origins which ignored a Creator. Even so, his theories were much criticized during his lifetime, and he sought to satisfy his critics in later editions of *The Origin of Species*.

The most serious problem he faced was the recognition of immense gaps in the fossil record. For instance, fossils representing complex and elaborate life forms were found suddenly appearing in the *Cambrian* geological strata with no transitional life forms. Darwin's response was merely a hope that later discoveries would provide "missing links." The missing links are still missing after 138 years. *There is not one single example of a convincing link between any basic kind and another kind.* Dr. Colin Patterson, a senior paleontologist at The British Museum of Natural History has written that if he knew of one transitional form he would have included it in some of his writing.[2] Darwin himself admitted if transitional forms were not found we should reject his theory, but evolutionists typically hang on to their *belief*. And why not? If one is unwilling to believe in a Creator, or if one is taught evolution as fact, or if one will be dismissed from his job as a teacher or investigator, it may be hard to deny.

Darwin saw no difficulty in claiming flying squirrels evolved into bats. Yet, bats possess many fantastic physical properties. They not only fly, but are

> **Reading Darwin's book today, one is struck by the lack of any scientific data, and Darwin's arguments are pure conjecture.**

nocturnal and fitted with a highly efficient sonar guidance system allowing them to hone in on flying insects. Each bat has his own recognizable clicks that make it possible to avoid neighboring bats in flight. The brain of the bat is specially developed in the auditory areas, and is capable of rapidly interpreting the signals received, enabling the bat to catch in flight thousands of insects every night. In addition to these extraordinary physical capabilities their body temperature, that is 100° to 105° F when fully active, falls to that of the environment when sleeping, conserving energy. Richard Leakey admits "unfortunately no fossils have yet been found of animals ancestral to the bats."[3]

> There is not one single example of a convincing link between any basic kind and another kind.

Darwin exhibits unscientific flights of fancy in a later paragraph: ". . . it is conceivable that flying fish, which now glide far through the air, slightly rising and turning by the aid of their fluttering fins, might have been modified into perfectly winged animals."[4]

Darwin saw no insurmountable difficulty with the eye forming itself by the aid of natural selection, despite the fact that we now know that the human eye handles a million bits of information per second. Biological processes seemed simple when knowledge was minimal.

First and Second Laws of Thermodynamics

These first and second laws of thermodynamics are two of the most certain, tested, and unforgiving laws of physical science.

The first of these laws deals with the conservation of energy. Energy can be converted from one form to another, but the total amount of energy remains unchanged; it is neither being created nor destroyed. This represents proof that there was a definite beginning to the physical universe, including earth and time.

The second law of thermodynamics makes the theory of evolution untenable, for it is accepted by physicists that although the total amount of energy remains constant, there is always a tendency for it to become less available for useful work. This is known as entropy, or randomness, or disorder, and "it will never, absolutely never become more ordered, more complex, more highly structured."[5] "There is a general tendency of all observed systems to go from order to disorder ... the law of increasing entropy."[6] "Another way of stating the second law, then is: 'The universe is constantly getting more disorderly!' ... In fact, all we have to do is nothing, and everything deteriorates, collapses, breaks down, wears out, all by itself — and that is what the second law is all about."[7]

Evolutionists have only a naive and totally inadequate answer, satisfactory only to their firm bias. We are all constantly made aware of the truth of the second law of thermodynamics which causes everything we know to decay, and proceed to come undone.

Notes

[1] Charles Darwin, *The Origin of Species by Means of Natural Selection* (New York: A.L. Burt Company, 1909), p. 424.

[2] Dr. Colin Patterson, Senior Paleontologist at the British Museum of Natural History in London, to Luther D. Sutherland; as quoted in *Darwin's Enigma* by Luther D. Sutherland (San Diego, CA: Master Books, 1984), p. 89.

[3] Richard E. Leakey, *The Illustrated Origin of Species* by Charles Darwin, Abridged and Introduced by Richard E. Leakey (New York: Hill and Wang, 1979), p. 128.

[4] Ibid., p. 106.

[5] Duane T. Gish, Ph.D., *Teaching Creation Science in Public Schools* (El Cajon, CA: Institute for Creation Research, 1995), p. 13.

[6] R.B. Lindsay, *American Scientist*, 56 (1968): 100.

[7] I. Asimov, *Smithsonian Institution Journal* (June 1970): 6.

REFLECTING ON LESSON ONE

1. What was Charles Darwin's academic background? Would it qualify him as an expert on the subject of biology?

2. What prior influences contributed to Darwin's formulating the theory he did? Who most readily accepted his theory, and why?

3. What is the difference between "evolution" and "variation within kinds"? Why is variation within kinds often termed "microevolution"? What did Darwin actually see in the Galapagos Islands?

4. What is the concept of "inheritance of acquired characeristics"? Has modern science confirmed or disproved this theory?

5. What did Darwin see as the main problem with his theory? Is it less of a problem or more of a problem today?

6. In what significant ways does a bat differ from a flying squirrel or lemur? What do you think the possibility would be that the necessary changes could just "happen"?

7. Summarize in your own words the first and second laws of thermodynamics. In what way does each conflict with the theory of evolution? How does the Christian belief in a Creator relate to these two laws?

2
T W O

WHY IS THE "THEORY" SO BAD?

Many of us are content, after being taught evolution theory, to work both sides of the street. Even Pope John Paul II, known to be theologically conservative on many issues, is attempting to take that approach.

On a theological basis, are you more willing to accept man's theories which change periodically and incessantly, or God's eternal Word which never changes? Happily, we are now blessed with much unbiased scientific knowledge that can test the Word. But before we turn to scientific facts, let us look at what havoc the theory of evolution has produced by those who would undermine what should be the sure foundation of God's truth.

Jesus said in John 8:12, "I am the light of the world; he that followeth me shall not walk in darkness, but shall have the light of life." Yet, evolutionist Theodosius Dobshansky quotes Pierre Teilhard de Chardin as claiming: "Evolution is a light which illuminates all facts, a trajectory which all lines of thought must follow."[1]

Our American forefathers believed God. George Washington said, "The whole duty of man is summed up in obedience to God's will." Noah Webster (1758-1843) was able to claim: "Education is useless without the Bible. The Bible is America's basic textbook in all fields." And Abraham Lincoln, on October 3, 1863 issued the proclamation of the first Thanksgiving: "[It is] announced in the Holy Scripture and proven by all history, that those nations are blessed whose God is the Lord. . . . God should be solemnly, reverently, and gratefully acknowledged . . . by the whole American people."

> "Evolutionary humanism is capable of becoming the germ of a new religion."
>
> —J. Huxley, atheist

Prior to the publication of Charles Darwin's book, *On the Origin of Species by Means of Natural Selection*, all clergy and most lay persons accepted God as Creator. With the publication of that book doubt was sown and atheists had their excuse to deny God, and their belief that they would never have to face Almighty God in the day of Judgment. Although Jesus had come to "free the captives," they believed they had received their freedom to do "what felt good." They were not going to give up this new freedom, and they were going to free society. Karl Marx was anxious to dedicate his book, *Das Kapital* to Darwin, but Darwin declined. Communists' first acts, when taking over a country have been to close the churches, and to teach evolution as doctrine.

Julian Huxley, atheist and prominent evolution spokesman, has written in *Evolution in Action*: "The word 'religion' is often used restrictively to mean belief in gods, but I am not using it in this sense . . . I am using it in a broader sense. . . . In this broad sense, *evolutionary humanism, it seems to me, is capable of becoming the germ of a new religion . . . .*"[2]

A new religion it has become, and the Humanist Manifesto II (1973) has infected our schools and universities. Paraphrased, it says:

1. No deity will save us; we must save ourselves.

2. Promises of immortal salvation, or fear of damnation are both illusory and harmful.

3. Ethics is autonomous and situational, needing no theological or ideological sanction.

4. Reason and intelligence are the most effective instruments that humankind possesses.

5. All religious, ideological, or moral codes that suppress freedom are rejected.

6. Individuals should be permitted to express their sexual proclivities, and life styles as they desire.

7. Civil liberties of all kinds are encouraged, including euthanasia.

8. Nationalism should be abandoned.

Paul Blanshard, a leading secular humanist, wrote in *The Humanist*, "I think the most important factor leading us to a secular society has been the educational factor. Our schools may not teach Johnny to read properly, but the fact that Johnny is in school until he is 16 tends toward the elimination of religious superstition. The average child now acquires a high school education, and this militates against Adam and Eve and all other myths of alleged history."[3]

Hitler was greatly influenced by the concepts of the infamous Ernst Haeckel and became an enthusiastic believer in evolution, applying its principles to the Nazi dogma. These principles were basic to his concept of the superiority of the Aryan race and his horrible program of destruction (known today as The Holocaust) of what he asserted to be "inferior" races.

Modern scientific knowledge contradicts the theory and philosophy of evolution, and it is imperative for us to know the facts, because it is not enough that we merely contend for our belief against their belief. We must teach our children because they are not learning the true scientific facts in school. The typical biology textbooks which I have personally critiqued are full of misrepresentations, claims which have been disproven but seldom recanted, and actual lies. I pray the following chapters will enlighten you, and supply you with the "sword of the Spirit, which is the word of God" (Eph. 6:17).

> Hitler was greatly influenced by the concepts of Ernst Haeckel and became an enthusiastic believer in evolution.

20

Quotes of Julian Huxley, Avid Evolutionist

"Evolutionary man can no longer take refuge from his loneliness by creeping for shelter into the arms of a divinized father-figure who he himself created, nor escape from the responsibility of making decisions by sheltering under the umbrella of Divine Authority, nor absolve himself from the hard task of meeting his present problems and planning his future by relying on the will of an omniscient but unfortunately inscrutable Providence."[4]

". . . Evolutionary Humanism is necessarily unitary instead of dualistic, affirming the unity of mind and body, . . . naturalistic instead of supernaturalist . . . . It will have nothing to do with Absolutes, including absolute truth, absolute morality, absolute perfection, and absolute authority, but insists that we can find standards to which our actions and our aims can properly be related."[5]

This is where the theory of evolution can ultimately lead.

---

[1] F.J. Ayala, *J. Heredity* 63:3 (1977).

[2] Julian Huxley, *Evolution in Action* (New York: Harper Brothers, 1953), p. 187.

[3] P. Blanshard, *Humanist*, March-April (1976), p. 17.

[4] Sir Julian Huxley, *Essays of a Humanist* (New York: Harper & Row, 1964), p. 125.

[5] Ibid., pp. 73-74.

REFLECTING ON LESSON TWO

1. Why do Christians try so hard to find a way for biblical creation and humanist evolution to work together?

2. Do you believe the theory of evolution has been a good and helpful theory for mankind, or that it undermines scriptural belief?

3. Discuss how Nazism and Communism, even though political opposites, have both leaned on evolutionary, humanistic principles.

4. Do you believe secular humanism has affected our schools and society? If so, in what ways, and are we doing enough in our schools?

5. Do you, right now, believe the theory of evolution must be true? If you found out it was untrue, what would you do about it?

4. What did George Washington advise? What did Noah Webster claim? Are these being taught in our schools and colleges, or would these teachings be explained away as being out of date and unnecessary?

5. How would you as a Christian respond to the quote by Pierre Teilhard de Chardin on page 18?

3
T H R E E

INSTITUTES FOR MISEDUCATION

For years after publication of *The Origin of Species* evolutionists accepted Darwin's claims that embryology, homology, and vestigial structures offered powerful substantiation of the theory of evolution. As science has replaced conjecture, practically all of these "evidences" have been abandoned by biological and embryological experts. Nevertheless the favorite claims persist in textbooks and teaching by those who have been taught what are now fabrications, or by those who refuse to let them die. Belief and bias prevail!

I was taught many of these false claims in medical school many years after they were shown to be false. The one which was most impressive was a flagrant lie promulgated by German zoologist Ernst Haeckel who became a staunch evangelist of Darwinism after reading his book. Haeckel falsified drawings of embryos, and presented them as evidence for recapitulation which he called "ontogeny recapitulates phylogeny," or "the biogenetic law." This catchy phrase purported that during embryonic development fish, mammals, and humans pass through all of the stages of ancestors. He falsified drawings by presenting the human head much smaller, and a tail significantly longer, and he claimed that ordinary folds in the neck represented gill slits.[1] The folds actually become thymus and parathyroid glands, and portions of the ear and lower jaw in mammals, but gills develop only in fish.

Haeckel's forgery and misrepresentation was recognized by embryologists, and he was accused, convicted, and denounced in 1874. Despite this the tale of recapitulation was taught as fact for years. The 1966, *Review Text in Biology*, "dedicated to serving our Nation's youth," taught, "Thus, we see the slit-like openings, called *gill slits*, in the neck region of all vertebrate embryos. . . . In addition to gill slits, such other organs as tails appear in all vertebrate embryos."[2] Though the gills are no longer claimed in 1996, textbooks still show what evolutionists claim to be similarity of embryos and it is surreptitiously suggested to students that this shows evidence of common ancestors. The fact is that human, fish, salamander, and chicken embryos are completely different in the very early blastula and gastrula stages of embryonic development. Any embryologist can easily spot the differences, and visualization of developing embryos using modern fetoscopes have proved that *human embryos are fully human from the beginning.*[3]

Haeckel's deceit, spread by "miseducation," has been indirectly responsible for the death of millions of innocent people. It was the "proof" Hitler used to justify, in his warped mind, the Holocaust with the slaughter of 6 million Jews whom he considered less "evolved" than Aryans. It was a significant "excuse" for the slaughter of thousands, and perhaps millions of Aborigines who were hunted down and shot in Australia. And the carnage goes on in abortion mills as women and girls are reassured that the life in their womb is a thing that is not yet human. How can we as a society allow this deception to continue? The biology textbooks used in our nation's schools are full of this kind of "miseducation."

Human embryos are fully human from the beginning.

In a debate with creationist Dr. Duane Gish, world famous Ashley Montagu made the following admission: "The theory of recapitulation was destroyed in 1921 by Professor Walter Garstang in a famous paper, since when no respectable biologist has ever used the theory of recapitulation, because it was utterly unsound, created by a Nazi-like preacher named Haeckel." When Dr. Gish stated that he is often confronted in debates with the recapitulation theory, Dr. Montagu replied, "Well, ladies and gentlemen, that only goes to show that many so-called educational institutions, called universities, are not educational institutions at all or universities; they are institutes for miseducation."[4] Recapitulation was taught to me as fact in medical school in 1943, and a facsimile is in our North Carolina approved biology textbooks today! Ladies and gentlemen, and mothers and fathers, Professor Montagu was talking about *our schools!*

Darwin and succeeding generations of evolutionists have tried hard for proof, but science continues to abort their theories.

The fossil record remained a disappointment to Darwin because it failed in his time to support his theory, and despite his fervent faith that transitional forms would eventually be found, knowledgeable evolutionists have been forced to admit they are absent. The same failure of faith has occurred regarding perhaps Darwin's most positive belief, i.e., homology. Homologous structures are those which appear the same in different animals or plants, but have different functions. I was taught that homology provided strong proof for evolution. Many textbooks still do. But, again, modern molecular biology disproves the concept.[5] Darwin believed this was powerfully suggestive of "inheritance from a common ancestor." Well, it certainly could be if it were so.

Sir Gavin de Beer, British embryologist and past Director of the British Museum of Natural History, writing in *Homology, an Unresolved Problem* concluded: "It is now clear that the pride with which it was assumed that the inheritance of homologous structures from a common ancestor explained homology was misplaced; for such inheritance cannot be ascribed to identity of genes." The attempt to find "homologous genes, except in closely related species, has been given up as hopeless."[6] The doctrine of homology, so prominently claimed by Darwin and preached by evolutionists, is totally without merit, and the teaching today of homology as evidence for evolution demonstrates either ignorance or deception.

As Conan Doyle wrote in *The Boscombe Valley Mystery*, "There is nothing more deceptive than an obvious fact."[7]

VESTIGIAL ORGANS

One other previously popular claim which has turned sour through scientific knowledge is the belief that vestigial organs and structures furnish evidence for descent from ancestors. Vestigial structures refer to those which, although useful in some, were considered useless or inconspicuous in others. At one time about 180 organs in the human body were considered to be useless vestiges. Here again ignorance of biology and embryology was responsible. With increasing knowledge, most of these are known to be useful in adults or during embryonic development. Among those now known to be highly useful but previously considered useless are the pineal gland, the thymus, the appendix and tonsils, which have immunologic function, and coccyx, which affords anchorage for pelvic muscles (once claimed to be a vestigial tail). Just because we can live without some of these organs does not imply they are useless. God supplies our needs with two eyes, two kidneys, two ovaries, two sets of teeth, etc. The placenta in mammals, and the allantois in birds and reptiles are vital during their embryonic stage. *Darwin and succeeding generations of evolutionists have tried hard for proof, but science continues to abort their theories.*[8]

The Amazing Monarch Butterfly

God must have made the Monarch Butterfly to prove to us that He is Creator. It is loaded with wonderful organs, physiology, and genetics. Its eyes are capable of seeing in all directions simultaneously, and it sees all the colors of the rainbow plus ultraviolet light. It has a navigation system capable of determining its position by relying on the earth's magnetic field and the position of the sun. This system weighs less than 0.5 grams, and is smaller than a pea. Its built-in instincts lead it to migrate from Mexico to Canada, although it has never before been

---

there. When winter approaches it migrates back to Mexico, sometimes returning to the same tree from which its migration began.

As an adult, the female lays eggs which hatch into caterpillars having three eyes capable of appreciating light from darkness, but no colors. An internal silk gland would be of no use to a butterfly, but after 17 days of constant eating the caterpillar spins a chrysalis (like cocoon), sheds its skin, head, and legs, and becomes enclosed in the chrysalis, blind and helpless. All internal organs liquefy except the beating heart which is the only moving part for eight days. The DNA is busy during this time directing the production of butterfly wings, legs, proboscis, and antennae, plus its remarkable butterfly eyes and little brain.

The morning of the eighth day brings forth the completed butterfly. It pumps fluid into the veins of its wings and flies away, guided by its little brain that interprets the guidance system and the preprogrammed instincts that lead it on its unique journey.

Can you really buy what evolutionists are selling – that this little creature is the product of no intelligent design, but rather unplanned, blind chance?

For more information about this fascinating insect, consult *From Darkness to Light to Flight*, by Jules H. Poirier, Institute for Creation Research, P.O. Box 2667, El Cajon, CA 92021.

---

[1] Michael Richardson, *Anatomy and Embryology*, August, 1997; see Elizabeth Pennisi, *Science* 277:1435 (1997). An article published in *The Times* of London, August 11, 1997, calls Haeckel an "embryonic liar."

[2] Mark A. Hall and Milton S. Lesser, *Review Text in Biology*, (New York: Amsco School Publications, 1966), pp. 366-367.

[3] Schwabenthan, *Parents*, October 1979, p. 50.

[4] Princeton University, April 12, 1980.

[5] Darwin, *The Origin of Species*, 6th ed. (New York: Collier Books, 1962), p. 434.

[6] Gavin de Beer, *Homology, an Unresolved Problem* (London: Oxford University Press, 1971), p. 16.

[7] Conan Doyle, "The Boscombe Valley Mystery," *The Complete Sherlock Holmes* (London: John Murray, 1928), p. 79.

[8] S.R. Scadding, "Do 'Vestigial Organs' Provide Evidence for Evolution?" *Evolutionary Theory* (May 1981): 5:173-176.

REFLECTING ON LESSON THREE

1. In what ways can a scientist's own bias (prior beliefs) affect his research? How has this affected the discussion of origins?

2. What is the "law" Haeckel taught concerning human and animal embryos? How long has the "law" been known to be false? Have you seen or heard of it being taught in the last 25 years?

3. What is homology? How has it been used as a "proof" of evolution? What modern understanding has shown that homology cannot be used as proof for evolution?

4. What did Sir Gavin de Beer claim about the concept of homology?

5. How did evolutionary theory influence Hitler? How has "miseducation" caused the death of millions today?

6. What are vestigial structures? What are some "vestigial" structures in the human body which have lately been shown to have very necessary purposes?

4
F O U R

YOUNG EARTH

In the "Christian" world, before Darwin, most people believed the earth and its inhabitants were created in six days, in the relatively recent past. Since Darwin the age of the earth has gradually increased through the changing minds of evolutionary uniformitarians who maintain that life and matter have developed by slow, natural, undirected processes. The age of the universe is now estimated by evolutionary geologists to be about 10-15 billion years and the earth 4.5 billion years.

Neither Creation nor evolution concepts are capable of being scientifically proven, because neither can be falsified. They are best considered to be models rather than theories. The Creation model, of course, requires belief in a Creator. Theologians have made a major mistake in attempting to correlate Scripture with what they consider to be science, when there is no scientific theory to agree with. Those of us who follow their example make a similar mistake.

Accommodation of the two models is impossible. The evolution model claims origins through millions of years of struggle and death. Would God claim this scenario to be "very good" (Gen. 1:31)? Furthermore, one of our most revered doctrines teaches that death resulted from man's sin. Dr.

Henry M. Morris and Henry M. Morris III point out there is also the problem regarding sedimentary rocks. Fossils are found in sedimentary rocks formed by the deposition of sediments by flowing water, which requires heavy rain.[1] Genesis 2:5-6 tells us there was no rain, "but there went up a mist from the earth that watered the whole face of the ground," until the Flood. How can the model of Creation be accommodated with the evolution model?

Recognizing the power of God, Creation could have occurred within seconds if He chose. When we start doubting God's word, there is nowhere in Scripture to stop doubting. God Himself told Moses in Exodus 20:11, "For in six days the Lord made heaven and earth, the sea, and all that in them is, and rested the seventh day." Certainly God knows what a day represents when spoken in this manner. Hebrew scholars agree that a twenty-four hour day is implied when, "the evening and the morning" are written, as in the days of the first chapter of Genesis. The phrases "evening and morning" occur over 100 times in the Old Testament, and always mean a twenty-four-hour day. Furthermore, in Genesis 1:14, if "day" is a long period of time the "signs, seasons, and years" are meaningless. As biological and geological information accumulates, Creation is authenticated, and evidence will show the theory of evolution is totally without foundation. We are not told exactly when Creation occurred, but scientific studies are yielding more and more evidence for a young earth.

The popular *evolutionary* model of how everything came to be from absolutely nothing is known as the "Big Bang." Because it is agreed there once was nothing, the idea begins (somehow) with a tiny bit of something (keeping it as close to nothing as possible) which explodes, scattering hydrogen atoms all over the universe. These hydrogen atoms are claimed to become, in at least 15 billion years, the galaxies and finally you and me!

Neither Creation nor evolution concepts are capable of being scientifically proven, because neither can be falsified.

30

An equally compelling difficulty with the Big Bang origin of the universe comes up against the Second Law of Thermodynamics. This law has never been negated, and it proclaims that everything in the universe is always becoming less organized. *An explosion will never, ever put itself back together, or create an organized product.* Organization requires plan, information, and energy. This second law of thermodynamics makes the evolution model scientifically impossible.

> An explosion will never, ever put itself back together, or create an organized product.

Evolutionists and geologists long ago grasped the high road and arbitrarily supplied names to the various rock layers and geologic ages. The naming of something gives to the thing a certain authority. Because the evolution model *requires* an ancient age, all of the strata of rocks and the enclosed fossils were given ancient ages in the 19th century. For instance, the stratum containing all of the known major invertebrate forms of life including corals, jellyfish, mollusks, sponges, crustaceans, and worms has been named Cambrian and given the beginning age 530 million years. The so-called Precambrian Period, if anything, contained only a few single-cell organisms, and yet the complex invertebrates claimed to be in the Cambrian Period were fully formed, with no intermediate transition forms to indicate evolution and no examples of ancestors.

It is possible to measure the amount of various chemicals and sediments passing into the oceans by the rivers of the earth. A uniformitarian table has been prepared by Drs. Henry M. Morris and Gary E. Parker, that brings together many different measurements. The figures are compiled from numerous sources available in *What Is Creation Science?*[2] There is great discrepancy in the ages determined, but all are far less than a billion years.[3]

Earth's magnetic fields have been decaying, and measurements monitored for many years indicate the age of earth to be significantly less than 20,000 years.[4]

Most meteors burn up in the earth's atmosphere, but a few land as meteorites into the geologic column. If the earth were 4.5 billion years old, meteorites should be easily found in great numbers. How many have been found? In a search of literature reported in June 1975 by P. Stevenson none had been found in the geologic column.[5]

Instead of requiring millions of years for coal to form from vegetation, as taught by evolutionists, *Dr. Robert Gentry has proved that coal can form in less than one year.* These findings have been confirmed by Professor Raphael Kazman of Louisiana State University, and by several other groups including scientists of Argonne National Laboratory. More recently researchers at Exxon published in the February 20, 1993 issue of *Science News* that oil can be rapidly produced by very hot water and organic material.

The mindset that causes us to want to believe our earth has always been more or less the same is called uniformitarianism. This is an old biased concept which it pleased Darwin to accept and foster in order to agree with his need for millions of years to account for life as we know it. However, Genesis 1:7 states: "And God made the firmament, and divided the waters which were under the firmament from the waters which were above the firmament: and it was so." This described the origin of a "Greenhouse effect" covering the entire earth. Three constituents, water vapor, ozone, and carbon dioxide would have been capable of maintaining a fairly constant temperature worldwide. Huge amounts of water vapor would have been available, because Genesis 2:5 includes the statement: "for the Lord God had not caused it to rain upon the earth, . . ." and Verse 6: "But there went up a mist from the earth, and watered the whole face of the ground."

> Dr. Robert Gentry has proved that coal can form in less than one year.

What would have been the effect of this "Greenhouse effect"? 1) There would have been a fairly constant temperature over the entire earth, and plenty of moisture to stimulate massive growth of vegetation. 2) There would have been huge quantities of water released during the great Flood. 3) Dragonflies with three-foot wingspreads have been found as fossils. These huge dragonflies would not have been capable of flying in our present-day atmosphere.

THE QUESTION OF EARLY MAN

Evolutionists still claim man evolved over thousands of years, yet *from the beginning man was highly intelligent,* and as skilled in many ways, or more so, than the present. For instance:

1) Genesis 11:6 (at Babel) "and the Lord said, Behold, the people are one, and they have all one language; and this they begin to do: and now nothing will be withheld from them, which they have imagined to do."

2) Over 4,000 years ago a Chinese developed the C Note of a musical instrument from which all notes of the musical scale were then mathematically derived.[6]

3) Ancient goldsmith work in Egypt dates from 4,000 years ago, and included electrolysis.[7]

4) 4,000 years ago Job spoke of writing or printing in a book (Job 19:23).

5) Electricity of one and one-half volts was produced in a ceramic jar containing a copper cylinder and iron core with the addition of grape juice. This was found in Ancient Mesopotamia.[8] This antedated Benjamin Franklin by thousands of years.

6) Pyramids were common in many areas such as Egypt, Mexico, and Central America. The first in Egypt (The Great Pyramid of Cheops) was of the best construction, and perhaps the largest ever built. The stones average two and one half tons, and are considered by some to be the finest cut stones ever produced. There has been minimal sag of the foundations, a compliment to the architects.[9]

7) Ancient Polynesians traveled over 15 million square miles of sea, navigating by the stars, and by techniques only recently rediscovered.[10]

8) The Mayans of Central America were very intelligent. Their year was calibrated 365.2420 days, compared to our very modern 365.2422 days![11]

9) The Mayans were able to move huge stones weighing up to 2,000 tons, an almost insurmountable task even using modern equipment.[12]

The evidence we now possess precludes any evidence that man has ever been anything but "modern man" in the "image of God."

SCIENTIFIC EVIDENCE FOR A SEVERAL-THOUSAND-YEAR AGE OF EARTH

Evolutionists have assumed the *uniformitarian principle,* that the cosmos, including earth, was formed by slow cooling of molten mass over 4.5 billion years to produce the granites that are the foundation rocks of the continents. The radioactive decay rate has been considered to be constant, the basis of long dating ages taught by evolutionists.

Dr. Robert V. Gentry is recognized as the preeminent world authority on Polonium halos, and he has worked extensively with zircons which are microscopic minerals that are often the centers of radioactive halos. Polonium-218 is a decay product of uranium in rocks with a half-life of only three minutes. However, the Polonium halos in the precambrian granites studied by Gentry showed no evidence of parent uranium which is an ordinary requirement. For a halo to appear in rock such as granite would require that the granite be almost instantly solidified. He wondered "were the polonium halos the fingerprints God left to identiy the Genesis rocks of our planet?"

To corroborate these findings he proceeded further to measure the content of helium within deep granites. Helium gas is a byproduct of uranium decay, and it diffuses out of zircons at a fairly rapid rate. Evolutionists had always considered it unnecessary to attempt measure of any residual helium content

The evidence we now possess precludes any evidence that man has ever been anything but "modern man" in the "image of God."

34

of zircons taken from deep granite cores, because it had been presumed that all, or almost all, helium should have migrated out of zircons during the billion or more years they were exposed to the higher temperatures of deep granites.

This experiment showed amazingly high retention of helium, and it is well known that helium would have been completely dissipated after long ages.

According to Dr. Gentry, these results provide overwhelming evidence, based on primordial polonium halos, for a several-thousand-year age of earth as opposed to a several-billion-year age. The several-billion-year age is scientifically incorrect.[13]

Work on primordial polonium halos provides overwhelming evidence for a several-thousand-year age of earth as opposed to a several-billion-year age.

[1] Dr. Henry M. Morris with Henry M. Morris III, *Many Infallible Truths* (Green Forest, AR: Master Books, 1996), p. 286.

[2] Henry M. Morris and Gary E. Parker, *What is Creation Science?* (San Diego, CA: Creation-Science Publishers, 1982).

[3] J.P. Riley and G. Skirrow, eds., *Chemical Oceanography* (New York, Academic Press, 1965), 1:164. See also Harold Camping, "Let the Oceans Speak," *Creation Research Society Quarterly*, Vol. II (June 1974): 39-45.

[4] John D. Morris, Ph.D., *The Young Earth* (Colorado Springs: Creation Life Publishers, Master Books Division, 1994), p. 74.

[5] P. Stevenson, "Meteorite Evidence for a Young Earth," *Creation Research Society Quarterly*, Vol. 12 (June 1975): 23.

[6] Dennis R. Petersen, *Unlocking the Mysteries of Creation* (El Dorado, CA: Creation Resource Foundation, 1986), p. 172.

[7] Ibid., p. 173.

[8] Ibid., p. 190.

[9] Ibid.

[10] Ibid., p. 188.

[11] Ibid., p. 192.

[12] Ibid., p. 194.

[13] Robert V. Gentry, D.Sc., Hon., *Creation's Tiny Mystery* (Knoxville, TN: Earth Science Associates, 1988), p. 170.

REFLECTING ON LESSON FOUR

1. Why can neither creation nor evolution be proven? Do you believe God might have used evolution to create?

2. According to the press we are told that the earth is 4.5 billion years old. Do you have proof that this is scientifically true?

3. Can you name at least two statements in Genesis 1 or 2 which contradict what the theory of evolution claims? Why is believing death is a result of sin cointradictory to evolution?

4. Many people claim a day of Genesis could be a thousand or more days. Do you agree, or does Scripture contradict this?

5. What is the Big Bang Theory? How do evolutionists explain what caused the Big Bang and where the matter produced by the Big Bang came from?

6. What are some of the various methods used for dating the age of the earth? What can be said about their reliability? How does Dr. Robert Gentry's work relate to other attempted dating methods?

7. Fossilized animals have been found in the arctic area with tropical vegetation in their stomachs. Can you explain this?

5

FIVE

THE FLOOD

"Knowing this first, that there shall come in the last days scoffers, walking after their own lusts, and saying, Where is the promise of His coming? For since the fathers fell asleep, all things continue as they were from the beginning of the creation. For this they willingly are ignorant of, that by the word of God the heavens were of old, and the earth standing out of the water and in the water, by which the world that then was, being overflowed with water, perished." 2 Peter 3:3-6.

Why do we have so much difficulty believing in the Noahic Flood? We seem naturally to believe the earth has always been like it is today. We also find ourselves in a period of adoration of "science" and faith in scientists. We overlook the fact that scientists have often come to wrong conclusions by bias and inadequate scientific methods. The earth was considered flat for centuries. Germs were unknown until discovered by Leeuwenhoek in 1687 and not recognized as a cause of infection until the middle of the 19th century. Darwin knew nothing about the power of genetics and variation within species as created by God. Today, bias is leading many, many scientists to battle against Creation, and I suspect most have never really studied the issues.

If we are open to believe Scripture, recent scientific evidence confirms a young earth and the Flood. It is essential that we accept the fact that the original world which God created was different in several respects as described in the second chapter of Genesis. This will take you to a world which evolutionists and some theologians have misrepresented.

Antiquity experts consider the Bible to be absolutely dependable in its historical facts. Many, many cultures of the world include histories of a worldwide flood, and yet evolutionary dogma, unfortunately supported by many theologians and taught in many seminaries, attempts to compromise belief with local floods or simple legend. However, factual evidence produced by godly scientists in the last 50 years supports a worldwide flood, the Flood of Noah. Actually, there are many facts of geology and origins which make no sense except through understanding the facts about the universal Flood and its consequences.

From Sunday school many of us have the idea that the Flood was produced by a gentle rain. *It was, in fact, a horrendous upheaval of the earth.* The "fountains of the great deep broken up" (Gen. 7:11) actually describes extreme violence with great volcanic activity, earthquakes, and likely vast tectonic movements of the earth's tectonic plates with release of huge amounts of subterranean water under extreme pressure. In addition, the "windows of heaven" (Gen. 7:11) spoke of "the waters which were above the firmament" (Gen. 1:7), and these waters were released.

Very few fossils of animals and plants are being formed at present. Flooding with waterborne sediment is by far the most common and efficient condition for producing fossils, because it is capable of rapid death and burial. As everyone knows, an animal dying in the sea or on the earth is promptly disposed of. As the sediment turns to rock, they tend to be permanently preserved as bone, or petrified, or as a mold or cast. The many layers of sedimentary rocks covering earth, including most mountaintops are teeming with billions and billions of

The flood was, in fact, a horrendous upheaval of the earth.

38

fossils. How can this be explained except by a universal, violent flood?

> There is plenty of evidence that some of the dinosaurs survived in the ark.

The Dinosaur National Monument located in Utah contains the disarticulated remains of more than 300 dinosaurs of various kinds. The appearance is of extreme violence, but also of preservation. Other sites of dinosaur destruction are found, such as that in the Gobi Desert, and about ten thousand duck-billed dinosaurs were fossilized together in Wyoming. Something big and powerful was obviously responsible for this mass destruction and burial. Could it have been anything but a global flood?

Evolutionists are unable to offer a satisfactory explanation for the demise of the dinosaurs. Does it not strike you as very strange and biased that none has suggested the Flood as the cause of the extinction of the dinosaur?

There is plenty of evidence that some of the dinosaurs survived in the ark, and that dinosaurs were known by man, but by other names. Remarkable accounts are described by Bill Cooper, B.A. (Hons).[1] He has gathered many episodes of "dragons" seen and described by numerous persons. (The name "dinosaur," meaning "terrible lizard," was first applied in the 1840s.) One such "reptilian monster" killed and devoured King Morvidus (Morydd) of Briton in 336 B.C. The monster "gulped down the body of Morvidus as a big fish swallows a little one." A table in Cooper's book lists 81 locations in the British Isles in which "reptilian monsters" have been reported, and he has accounted for 200, some of which are dated to the comparatively recent past.

Two such monsters, Behemoth and Leviathan, are described in the Book of Job (Job 40:15-24 and 41:1-34).

Dinosaurs did not die out 65 million years ago. Rock walls in South America, Africa, China, Australia, Europe, and North America were decorated by men with images of dinosaurs.[2]

THE GRAND CANYON

The Grand Canyon is an excellent example of the effects of the Flood, and the striking error that evolutionary thinking has fostered. It has been taught for years that the Colorado River carved out the Canyon during millions of years. This claim has many faults. For one, the Colorado River now passes through a large mountain range at the beginning of the Grand Canyon. Rivers do not readily pass through mountain ranges. The Canyon is twenty miles wide and 200 miles long, and there is no delta downstream despite trillions of acres of soil washed away. The rock walls show no evidence of erosion, and a knife cannot be passed between rock layers. Evidence strongly suggests that two huge lakes (which have been named Grand and Hopi Lakes), which contained as much water following the Flood as the combined existing Great Lakes, broke through the mountain range dam and within weeks washed out the freshly laid rock layers left by Noah's Flood.[3] The catastrophic flow dissipated material all over the southwestern states, leaving no delta which would be expected if there had been slow erosion.

"THE TABLE OF NATIONS"

Evolutionists and many theologians persist in considering the "Table of Nations" recorded in the 10th chapter of Genesis as being either myth or inconclusive. The theory of evolution and the 10th chapter of Genesis can have no agreement. *The Genesis record agrees with the young earth, and the theory of evolution is dead in the water if millions of years cannot be proved.*

Bill Cooper, author of *After the Flood,* has obtained absolute proof through careful search of recorded history of early British kings, Anglo-Saxon kings, Danish and Norwegian kings, Irish Celtic kings, and ancient chronologies that the recorded history of Genesis chapter 10 is factual and trustworthy.

The Grand Canyon is an excellent example of the effects of the Flood.

The descent of six Anglo-Saxon Royal Houses began with Noah-Sceaf (pagan Saxon name for Japheth)-Bedwig-Hwala, etc. The genealogies of the

Norwegians, Danes, Icelanders, and English Saxons began with Noa-Seskef or Sceaf (Japheth)-Bedwig-Hwala, etc. The Irish Celtic list begins with Noah-Japheth-Magog, etc.

The proof rests in the fact that these people were not privy to the Bible for 100 to 1000 years. Furthermore, the records were carefully guarded and the rights of succession rested on them. Fraud or forgery would have been dealt with decisively. They all kept account of time and considered the earth to have

> The Genesis record agrees with the young earth, and the theory of evolution is dead in the water if millions of years cannot be proved.

been created about 5,200 years B.C. and the Flood 2,242 years after Creation. These figures agree significantly with the Mayans, who were halfway around the earth and who had knowledge about the Flood but dated it to 3113 B.C.

Folks, we live on a young earth!

There seems to be no way to overcome the bias of evolutionists.

CONCLUSION

It is apparent that all or most of the fossil rock layers were deposited during the Noahic Flood. The so-called geologic column was conceived in bias and lack of scientific evidence, and produces confusion. I urge creationists to name geologic layers for the predominant class or classes of organisms found, rather than continuing to use the unreasonable, evolutionary names that suggest to the reader millions of years. The evolution model has claimed stratigraphic succession order as demonstrating succeeding evolutionary ages of fossils when in reality the order can best be explained as relating to hydrodynamic selectivity (size, weight, and shape of organisms), differential escape (abilities of organisms to move), and ecological zonation (where the organisms lived). Thus, clams would be expected to be found in fossil deposits lower than mammals even though buried by the Flood in the same year.

[1] Bill Cooper, B.A. (Hons), *After the Flood* (Chichester, West Sussex, England: New Wine Press, 1995), Chapter 10.

[2] John D. Morris, Ph.D., *Dinosaurs, The Lost World, and You* (El Cajon, CA: Institute for Creation Research, 1997), p. 26.

[3] Walt Brown, *In the Beginning: Compelling Evidences for Creation and the Flood*, 6th ed. (Phoenix, AZ: Center for Scientific Creation, 1995), pp. 94, 103-105.

It is apparent that all or most of the fossil rock layers were deposited during the Noahic Flood.

REFLECTING ON LESSON FIVE

1. Why have you had difficulty believing in the Noahic Flood?

2. Describe the geologic and meteorologic events which took place at the time of the flood. What do many researchers think the earth and its atmosphere were like before the flood?

3. What evidences exist that dinosaurs still roamed the earth after man came on the scene?

4. What method could account for finding progressively complex fossils in higher layers of sedimentary rock if not evolution?

5. What is a fossil? How does a fossil form? How do you believe a huge dinosaur became a fossil? How do you believe the dinosaurs died?

6. When you look at the vertical walls of the canyon, does it seem more reasonable to believe the Grand Canyon was formed by the Colorado River over millions of years, or by rapid water flow?

7. What facts described by Bill Cooper offer significant reassurance to you that the 11th chapter of Genesis is true?

6
S I X

WILL YOU BET AGAINST GOD?

In olden times it was considered reasonable to believe that life came from nonlife by naturalistic means. Everybody could see that mold grew on stale bread, fruit flies appeared on rotting fruit, and maggots infested decaying meat. However, the great French scientist *Louis Pasteur proved what we now recognize as the **law of biogenesis** — that life arises only from pre-existing life.* He sterilized a nutritious fluid by boiling, and sealed the container to keep out all microbes. No living organisms appeared. This same process is now called *pasteurization,* and is a guaranteed process which has been used ever since to thwart germs.

In a lecture Pasteur reported: Never will the doctrine of spontaneous generation recover from the mortal blow of this simple experiment."[1] Yet evolutionists claim it did happen, "Once upon a time," despite impossible odds. Pasteur's experiments and today's scientific knowledge are absolutely logical and mathematically unimpeachable, and yet evolutionists' best hope is held in a remarkably flawed experiment by Stanley Miller in 1953.

Miller chose an "atmosphere" of hydrogen, methane, ammonia, and water vapor, knowing that oxygen would destroy any amino acids (some of the building blocks of life). He then exposed the gases to electric sparks to simulate lightning. A few amino acids plus several other insignificant compounds formed. Evolutionists bet the farm on this.

Science? Life requires 20 special essential amino acids. Living proteins also require that all of these 20 be so-called "levo (left) racemates," which relate to the way the carbon, oxygen, and hydrogen atoms are arranged. In inorganic nature one-half of amino acids are right-handed and one-half are left-handed. It would only take one right-handed amino acid to ruin a protein molecule. Only a cell with its contained DNA and special proteins can make proteins with 100% levo forms. Evolutionists do not talk or write in their textbooks about this little problem. The word "racemate" does not appear in any North Carolina approved biology textbook that I have examined.

To function properly the sequence of amino acids in a protein must be absolutely perfect. A single "wrong" amino acid may cause severe problems. Sickle cell anemia, a serious blood disease, is caused by a single mistake — a mutation. The amino acid valine replaces glutamic acid, one out of 574 amino acids in the protein molecule of hemoglobin.

The odds against life appearing spontaneously on earth at any time are ridiculously high — in the zone of complete absurdity. The simplest living organism known is the very small, bacteria-like Mycoplasma hominis H39. It has about 500 different protein molecules, each composed of an average of 400 amino acids. Remember, each protein must have its amino acids in an exact sequence to function.

The probability of obtaining the correct sequence of just one molecule of protein has been estimated to be one in 10^{520} or 10 followed by 520 zeros! Don't forget, there are 500 proteins and the amino acids must all be levo shaped. Give up? I suspect the great majority of those who accept the theory of evolution are not aware of these facts and odds. The textbooks do not point this out, and the teachers are not teaching it.

There is no such thing as life without a cell. Also, there is no such thing as "simple" life, because the smallest of bacteria must digest food for energy, excrete waste, and reproduce — and be alive. The modern electron microscope has supplied us with pictures of the complexity of the living cell and its "organelles," which are little factories within the cell. The cell membrane looked like a plastic wrapper in the old light microscope, but now we see that the cell membrane is composed of active proteins and fat molecules. These regulate passage of substances in and out of the cell. Some cell membranes have active flagella attached, which rotate by the power of an electron motor to produce motion. Have you ever heard of an electric motor that made itself?

The enclosing cell membrane is absolutely vital to the functions of the cell and for the physiological activities of the organism. The membrane is semipermeable, allowing free passage in and out for some molecules such as oxygen and carbon dioxide. But the movement of potassium and calcium is regulated. This requires energy, plan, and organization. A very important function is immunological, protecting the cell from invasion by toxins, viruses, and bacteria.

It is axiomatic that life cannot exist in the absence of a fully functional cell membrane, and it is equally axiomatic that a "sophisticated" cell membrane cannot be brought into being except by a living cell! Evolutionists never try to answer this dilemma, because there is only one answer that fits: creation.

Life is a machine. As stated earlier, the DNA enclosed within chromosomes (46 in humans) is the blueprint for the design of the body and for the physiological functions. It resides in the nucleus of the cell. Other organelles include ribosomes, which manufacture proteins (with the aid of other proteins); centrioles, which are important in cell division; mitochondria, which are responsible for energy conversion for the cell; Golgi complexes, which store and refine special secretory products; and lysosomes, which digest

The enclosing cell membrane is absolutely vital to the functions of the cell and for the physiological activities of the organism.

46

organic food compounds and remove undesirable substances such as dead bacteria, viruses, and worn-out components of the cell. Secretory granules, composed of enzymes, hormones, and immune globulins are stored in the cytoplasm of the cell.

Through God's ingenuity, animals and plants use each other's byproducts in a perfect relationship.

The cell wall of plants is reinforced with cellulose to provide rigidity for upright growth. Plant cells are otherwise similar to animal cells except for the presence of chloroplasts within which chlorophyll, utilizing the energy of sunlight converts carbon dioxide plus water into glucose. Oxygen is a byproduct. *Through God's ingenuity, animals use oxygen for life, and carbon dioxide is produced as a byproduct. Plants use carbon dioxide to produce food and oxygen for animals — a perfect relationship.*

The invention of chlorophyll and photosynthesis rivals the miracle of life. *Those who hold the implausible possibility of the origin of life by chance alone must add the simultaneous origin of photosynthesis.* Nobody knows exactly how photosynthesis works, but it is a very complicated process requiring special genes, chlorophyll, proteins, and several chemical agents including quinone, pheophytin, and cytochrome. Evolutionists explain how it developed by simply claiming it "evolved," their answer for everything.

---

[1] R. Valery-Radot, *The Life of Pasteur* (New York: Dover Publications, 1960), p. 109.

[2] Darwin, *Origin of Species* 6th ed., p. 154.

[3] Michael J. Behe, *Darwin's Black Box* (New York: The Free Press, A Division of Simon & Schuster, 1996), p. 39.

47

Irreducible Complexity

Darwin admitted: "If it could be demonstrated that any complex organ existed which could not possibly have been formed by numerous, successive, slight modifications, my theory would absolutely break down."[2] Natural selection plays an essential role in Darwinian evolution, and it could only "choose" systems that are functioning.

Michael J. Behe, in *Darwin's Black Box* defines *irreducible complexity* as a "single system composed of several well-matched, interacting parts that contribute to the basic function, wherein the removal of any one of the parts causes the system to effectively cease functioning."[3]

There are many complex systems in various organisms which could be cited as being irreducibly complex. These include various types of eyes, the human brain, and the kidneys. Of special interest are the several kinds of bacteria which are propelled by a flagellum which rotates by an electric motor. The motor is firmly seated in the wall of the bacterium, and the rotor is powered by a very complicated electronic device which has not yet been completely elucidated, despite much research.

Besides falling into Behe's definition of irreducible complexity, whoever saw or even heard of a motor which made itself?

Those who hold the implausible possibility of the origin of life by chance alone must add the simultaneous origin of photosynthesis.

48

REFLECTING ON LESSON SIX

1. How did Pasteur's work demonstrate a fundamental law of science? What can we conclude from this about the question of human origins?

2. What did Stanley Miller produce in 1953? Why have evolutionists claimed this as proof of life developing from nonlife? Is there any merit in these claims?

3. What is the basic structure of any living thing? Is the component makeup of this structure simple or complex?

4. What is the function of a cell membrane?

5. What are proteins made of? What happens if the sequences of amino acids in proteins are not 100% correct? What else is needed for proper proteins to exist? What is a racemate?

6. What is special about plant cells? Would life on earth be possible without plants?

7. What is irreducible complexity? Are you aware of any biological organs which fall in this category?

7
S E V E N

VARIATION: GOD'S PLAN AND EVOLUTION'S FALSE CLAIM

Evolutionists claim that bacteria and blue-green algae were the first organisms, called prokaryotes. Prokaryotes lack a true nucleus, and multiply by asexual division or cloning (mitosis) in which one cell splits its genetic material, and two cells are produced. All other forms of life, both plants and animals, are so-called eukaryotes which multiply by sexual reproduction. In this, the parent organisms (male and female) each supply one half of the genetic material. Thus, each new individual is unique, because the "genetic material" is really DNA, contained within genes, and which represents the blue-print of the new cell. The reproductive mechanism is totally different in prokaryotes from that of eukaryotes.

The cell structure of prokaryotes and eukaryotes is also vastly different. In eukaryotes the genetic material is contained in a nucleus within the cells, and the eukaryotic cell contains many different kinds of so-called "organelles" which are little factories containing protein machines.

Some bacteria in a population contain plasmids, which are circular DNA molecules and may be transmitted among prokaryotes. These plasmids are especially important in the transfer of antibiotic resistance, which is not mutation or errors of transcription, but actual introduction of widely distributed information among prokaryotes. It is limited to prokaryotes. The DNA in prokaryotes forms a single chromosome, and there are no true membrane-enclosed organelles. *Evolutionists and your public school biology textbooks claim that prokaryotes "evolved" into eukaryotes, but they have no satisfactory explanation how this remarkable change occurred.*

> Textbooks claim that prokaryotes "evolved" into eukaryotes, but they have no satisfactory explanation how this remarkable change occurred.

Roger Y. Stanier, microbiologist with the Institut Pasteur, Paris, France stated: ". . . the structural differences between eukaryotic and prokaryotic cells are expressive of highly important differences in the way that universal cell functions are accomplished: Notably the transmission and expression of genetic information, the performance of energy metabolism, and the entry and exit of materials. It is evident that the line of demarcation between eukaryotic and prokaryotic cellular organisms is the largest and most profound single evolutionary discontinuity in the contemporary biological world."[1]

In other words, they are very, very different. Darwin wrote, "If it could be demonstrated that any complex organ existed which could not possibly have been formed by numerous, successive, slight modifications, my theory would absolutely break down. But I can find out no such case."[2] This is such a case! Yet evolutionists pass over this with a semantic "evolved." No attempt is made to explain *how* it might have evolved.

I believe God created the concept of sexual reproduction for at least two very important reasons. The first was looking forward to the family under God, with the children sharing the genes of both parents, and each individual being unique. The second important reason was to allow this uniqueness to produce variation within kinds. Variation within kinds results in the fine-tuning of physical and physiological mechanisms to adjust for changes in our environment. Note! It is extremely important to understand that no new or additional information in the form of DNA is added. *It just produces different proportions or different expressions of the same old genetic material.*

As usual, Satan has misused this blessed creation for his purposes, and he has used it to foster the theory of evolution. Darwin and his contemporary, Alfred Russel Wallace, and evolutionists ever since were led down a primrose lane by the differences within kinds resulting in variations. Darwin, who sailed to the Galapagos Islands on board H.M.S. Beagle, was greatly impressed by the differences in the beaks of various finches, and the differences in the shells of tortoises located on various islands. After his return home to England he continued observations in the breeding of animals (especially pigeons) and plants, and became convinced that living things change over time. He reasoned that "natural selection" through extended time would result in those which are best suited to the environment becoming dominant in the struggle to survive. Lacking knowledge of genetics, Darwin failed to recognize simple variation within kinds. Scientists and teachers of today should certainly know the difference between variation within kinds (no new DNA) and entirely different kinds (new and different DNA).

God tells us in the first chapter of Genesis that He created "after their kinds," and He tells us this ten times. Do you suppose He knew Satan was going to try to weaken belief in His word, and this is His warning? Satan, knowing that man is easily led to believe what he wants to believe, has convinced many that variation leads, over time, to new kinds. It becomes a belief. Everything that Darwin saw and everything that he described involved variation within kinds. Unfortunately, there is a lot of ignorance (or possibly misrepresentation) because the textbooks and other presentations by evolutionists are full of variations within kinds, intended to represent examples of evolution.

Variation within kinds produces different proportions or different expressions of the same old genetic material.

52

We see variations within kinds all the time, both in nature and in the results of plant and animal breeding. But there are limits to what breeding can accomplish. Evolutionists have invented a semantic way to confuse the unenlightened by calling variations "microevolution." The so-called macroevolution has never been demonstrated, but to them it is possible to imagine change plus natural selection doing the job. I urge you to be very careful, and use your mind when you read or see their material. DNA is the blueprint or code for each kind of plant or animal, and as we will discuss in the next chapter, elegant new structures cannot be coded by a misprint called mutation. A child tampering with your cake recipe or a blueprint for a house or airplane is not going to make it better.

A giraffe's neck requires exceptionally high blood pressure and special valves in the arteries of the brain

We have to be very careful not to credit variation rather than special creation too glibly. In the days of Darwin and the entire 19th century, very little was known about molecular biology and of physiology related to anatomy. It was easy to postulate giraffes gradually growing longer necks. But now we know that the long neck *requires exceptionally high blood pressure to pump blood to the brain when it reaches up for food, and special valves in the arteries of the brain* able to close to prevent the blood from engorging the brain when the head is lowered to drink. The more we learn about biology, the more we are led to see God's glory.

We continually see variations among dogs, cats, people, and all kinds of animals and plants. Darwin mistakenly based his theory on variations within kinds which he saw among finches, tortoises, and lizards in the Galapagos Islands, and in his breeding experiments. But he was wrong, and evolutionists continue to be wrong in their claims.

This error is the greatest problem we face in trying to understand each other. Darwin got things off to a false start, not having access to Gregor Mendel's groundbreaking research in genetics, nor our present knowledge of DNA and cellular biochemistry.

---

[1] Roger Y. Stanier, Edward A. Adelburg, John L. Ingraham, Mark L. Wheelis, *Introduction to the Microbial World* (Englewood Cliffs, NJ: Prentiss-Hall, 1979), p. 46.

[2] Leakey, *Illustrated Origin of Species*, p. 128.

Bombardier Beetle

Duane T. Gish, Ph.D., Senior Vice President and Professor of Natural Science at the Institute for Creation Research in Santee, California, loves to debate evolutionists, and he enjoys telling about the unique and effective defense mechanism of the bombardier beetle. Evolutionists are quite unable to explain how this fascinating beetle developed by evolutionary means. It is another example of irreducible complexity.

When threatened, the bombardier beetle fires hot (212° F), smelly liquid and gases into the face of the enemy. The mechanism consists of twin storage chambers and twin combustion tubes which point posteriorly. Solutions of two chemicals, 10% hydroquinone and 23% hydrogen peroxide, are stored in the two chambers. When alarmed, the chemical solutions are passed into the combustion tubes where two enzymes, catalase and peroxidase, are added. The reaction is explosive, providing high pressure, heat to 212°, stench, and irritation to the offender when the combustion tubes are opened and the steam released.

Dr. Gish points out that *if every phase were not perfect from the beginning the bombardier beetle would have blown himself up!*

If every phase of its defense mechanism were not perfect from the beginning the bombardier beetle would have blown itself up.

54

REFLECTING ON LESSON SEVEN

1. What are prokaryotes and eukaryotes? How do they differ? Why would one evolving to become the other be unlikely?

2. Why did God create the concept of sexual reproduction? From a social perspective? From a biological perspective?

3. What three-word phrase, used ten times in Genesis 1, refutes the idea of macroevolution? What evidences for macroevolution have been found?

4. Why do you think Darwin did not know the difference between evolution and variation within kinds? Why do you think many scientists do not recognize the difference?

5. Why would a giraffe suffer if he became a giraffe simply by gradually growing a long neck?

8
E I G H T

PALEONTOLOGY'S "TRADE SECRET"

According to American humorist Artemus Ward, "It ain't so much the things we don't know that gets us in trouble. It's the things we know that ain't so."

Darwin's theory was based on the premise that all living things evolved over vast periods of time by slow change in forms, through chance, and guided by natural selection. He had bulldog faith in his theory, even though he had to defend his theory against many detractors. He also had lots of supporters. It was a time when many were believing in the power of humanism, and that man was innately good with potential for progress in all things. Rationalism prevailed. Darwin had studied for the ministry, and he had a Christian wife, but he had declined ordination to the clergy, recognized his own spirituality as muddled, and in his writings to family and friends he called himself agnostic. He suffered much from chronic abdominal distress.

The most serious problem he faced was the realization that the fossil record did not support his theory. There were no bona fide transitional forms indicating change of one kind to another, i.e. no half-fish/half-amphibian, nor half-reptile/half-bird. There were also groups of kinds suddenly appearing. He recognized these as crucial, but he kept the faith that the fossil record would eventually redeem itself. He wrote: "The abrupt manner in which whole groups of species suddenly appear in certain formations has been urged as a fatal objection to the belief in the transmutation of species. If numerous species belonging to the same genera or families have really started into life at once, the fact would be fatal to the theory of evolution through natural selection . . . . But we continually overrate the perfection of the geological record . . . ."[1]

> Darwin said that if the fossil record failed to confirm his theory, it should be considered dead.

Note that *Darwin said that if the fossil record failed to confirm his theory, it should be considered dead.* But it isn't. Evolutionists simply keep right on declaring the fossil record confirms evolution. Check your child's public school textbook! Others, like Stephen Jay Gould, world famous paleontologist at Harvard, resurrects the theory with a theory of his own, which is by no means accepted by all evolutionists. Gould has stated: "The extreme rarity of transitional forms in the fossil record persists as the trade secret of paleontology — Darwin's argument still persists as the favored escape of most paleontologists from the embarrassment of a record that seems to show so little of evolution directly — it was never 'seen' in the rocks."[2]

G.G. Simpson, paleontologist of Columbia University, confirms Gould, writing: "The regular absence of transitional forms is not confined to mammals, but is an almost universal phenomenon, *as has long been noted by paleontologists*" (emphasis mine).[3]

The problem evolutionists run into is simply that evolution of one kind to another kind hasn't happened. The fossil record has always shown remarkable stasis of kinds. Bees are known to have changed very little. Cockroaches, dragonflies, starfish, bacteria, Ginkgo trees, sharks, and many other common organisms of today are essentially unchanged from fossils claimed to be 200 to 600 million years old.

Austin Clark of the U.S. National Museum, who spent many

years investigating the relationships of various groups of animals to each other, both fossil and living, affirmed in *The New Evolution Zoogenesis* that there had been no change in the interrelationships of the phyla or major groups of animals since life first began.[4] He added: ". . . the whales and the seals are always whales and seals, and show little or no approach to any other type of mammal. . . . A backboned animal is always unmistakably a backboned animal, a starfish is always a starfish, and an insect is always an insect no matter whether we find it as a fossil or catch it alive at the present day."[5]

It appears Dr. Clark affirms through years of research what Genesis chapter one declares ten times: that God created after their kinds. Paul affirms in I Corinthians 15:39, "All flesh is not the same flesh: but there is one kind of flesh of men, another flesh of beasts, another of fishes, and another of birds."

In 1984 Luther D. Sunderland interviewed five leading paleontologists associated with several of the largest natural history museums in the world. He summarized their opinions as follows: "*None of the five museum officials could offer a single example of a transitional series of fossilized organisms* that would document the transformation of one basically different type to another." He quoted Dr. Niles Eldredge, curator of Invertebrate Paleontology at the American Museum in New York, NY, admitting that people are fed up with "imaginary stories," and that ". . . an awful lot of that has gotten into the textbooks as though it were true. For instance, the most famous example still on exhibit downstairs (in the American Museum in New York) is the exhibit on horse evolution prepared perhaps 50 years ago. That has been presented as literal truth in textbook after textbook. Now I think that is lamentable, particularly because the people who propose these kinds of stories themselves may be aware of the speculative nature of some of the stuff. But by the time it filters down to the textbooks, we've got science as truth and we've got a problem."[6]

Not one of five museum officials interviewed by Luther Sunderland could offer a single example of a transitional series of fossilized organisms.

The "problem" is still on exhibit downstairs, and still prominently displayed in all of the North Carolina approved textbooks which I have examined. The cure would be to start teaching the truth to our children, and yet several state legislatures have turned down attempts to do just that because of pressure by evolutionist groups.

Snake "Eyes"

Irreducible complexity is not the only scientific analysis which strains beyond belief Darwin's theory of evolution by natural selection. Composite, simultaneous origin of a complex living system is perhaps an even more convincing example of intelligent design.

An example described authoritatively in the March 1982 edition of *Scientific American* titled, "The Infrared 'Vision' of Snakes"[7] is a striking case in point. The poisonous pit vipers (subfamily Crotalinae), including North American rattlesnakes, copperheads, and cottonmouth moccasins, are the only poisonous snakes which are armed with heat-sensitive pits which open below and in front of both eyes.

The pits are constructed with a very thin membrane containing numerous sensory nerves. The membrane is suspended in air on both sides with the obvious purpose of avoiding the loss of heat to deeper tissues. If the nerves only recorded a warm face, it would be of no special use. The nerves, however, carry the sensation to a special nerve center peculiar to these snakes, and from there the impulses travel to a special nucleus located in the hindbrain, and thence the impulses are projected to a very important nerve center in the brain called the optic tectum. The tectum is the main center for processing information such as sight and sound for the localization of objects in space.

Through this system the pit viper can localize a mouse or other critter in the dark with an accuracy of 5 degrees. Pythons and some other nonpoisonous members of the family Boidae also have heat-sensitive pits, but their system is different in several significant ways.

The authors who meticulously worked out the knowledge of this incredibly complex system claim it evolved! One wonders if they really believe it evolved, or whether it was essential to claim evolution to have the material published in *Scientific American*. The system "evolved" from nowhere, and "evolved" to nowhere. It is quite unique.

---

[1] Darwin, *Origin of Species*, pp. 333-334.

[2] Stephen Jay Gould, *The Panda's Thumb* (New York, London: W.W. Norton and Co., 1980), p. 181.

[3] G.G. Simpson, *Tempo and Mode in Evolution* (Morningside Heights, NY: Columbia University Press, 1944), p. 106.

[4] Austin H. Clark, *The New Evolution Zoogenesis* (Baltimore: The Williams and Wilkins Co., 1930), p. 104.

[5] Ibid., p. 167.

[6] Luther D. Sunderland, *Darwin's Enigma: Fossils and Other Problems* (Santee, CA: Master Book Publishers, 1984), p. 78.

[7] Eric A. Newman and Peter H. Hartline, "The Infrared 'Vision' of Snakes," *Scientific American* (March 1982): 14-23.

REFLECTING ON LESSON EIGHT

1. Do you think Darwin would continue to support his own theory today if he could see the scientific evidence which has been compiled in the last 100 years? Why or why not?

2. If evolution were true, what would we expect to find in the fossil record? If creation by God is true, what should we find? In fact, what do we find?

3. What did Austin Clark, head of the U.S. National Museum, say about the animals? What did the apostle Paul say?

4. Did world-famous paleontologists offer Luther D. Sunderland examples of transitional forms proving evolution to be true?

5. Is the famous "horse series" true? Do you believe the "horse series" should continue to be shown in museums and textbooks?

6. How can we solve the problem of Paleontology's "Trade Secret"?

9

N I N E

MUTATIONS: MAGIC?

The ultimate engine of the theory of evolution is claimed to be mutation. I am not talking about variations within kinds, which evolutionists keep calling evolution (or microevolution, if pushed). I am talking about increasing complexity resulting first in life from nonlife, eukaryotes from prokaryotes, multicelled organisms from single-celled organisms, lungs from gills, feathers from scales, etc.

In this lesson I want you to put on your thinking cap and ponder. Every organism, including you, is made from a blueprint called DNA, which is short for deoxyribonucleic acid. DNA is basically a complex chemical compound which is stable, and also carefully protected, and which acts like a Morse code.

The DNA code for a small bacterium like E. coli is representative of about three million code "words," which is comparable to three books of 1,000 pages with 1,000 words per page. That is a lot of information! Your DNA is estimated to represent three *billion* code "words," which would fill 3,000 volumes of 1,000 pages with 1,000 words per page.

Incidentally, the DNA strand is folded, and there is a complete strand in each cell of your body, distributed in and composing the genes. This works on average for over 70 years with no known extraneous intellect guiding its decisions! Evolutionists believe this incredible code came into existence by undirected, pure chance!

The DNA is the absolute blueprint for whatever the cell design is, and for all of the processes which the cell does, including the molecular activities. This includes cell production, cellular digestion, immune mechanisms, detoxification, manufacture of hundreds and thousands of proteins, *ad infinitum*. Nothing conceptual can occur that is not dependent on DNA, and so for a bird to change from a reptile or dinosaur would require thousands or millions of highly technical mutations, yielding increased genetic material.

Well, what is a mutation anyway? *A mutation is a misprint or defective copy of DNA.* Reproduction of an organism involves the replication of the DNA contained in sex cells. Most misprints are corrected by special proteins that help the replication process, and a high percentage of the few misprints are of no great significance. Major genetic misprints, however, are best considered always harmful.

J.J. Freidn states in *The Mystery of Heredity*: "We have to face one particular fact, one so peculiar that in the opinion of some people it makes nonsense of the whole theory of evolution; although the biological theory calls for incorporation of beneficial variance in the living populations, a vast majority of the mutants observed in any organism are detrimental to welfare. Some are lethal, causing incurable diseases or fetal deaths; others are sub-lethal, killing off or incapacitating most of the carriers, or allowing some to escape; still others are sub-vital, damaging health, resistance or vigor in a variety of ways."[1]

C.P. Martin of McGill University has written: "The mass of evidence shows that all or almost all known mutations are unmistakably pathological and the few remaining ones are highly suspect."[2]

A mutation is a misprint or defective copy of DNA.

Are you convinced that there are no conceivable methods known by which significant changes can develop to produce new organs or hormones or

62

kinds? If not, read what Theodosius Dobzhansky, evolutionist and renowned naturalist who has done extensive work subjecting fruit flies to radiation in order to produce mutation, has said. "The clear-cut mutants . . . are almost without exception inferior to wild-type flies in viability, fertility, and longevity. Mutation never produced anything new. They had malformed wings, legs and bodies, and other distortions, but they always remained fruit flies . . . ."[3]

> You would not expect a five-year-old child to dabble in a blueprint for the construction of an airplane, and make it better.

H.J. Muller, recipient of the Nobel Prize for his work with mutation, stated, "Most mutations are bad. In fact good ones are so rare that we can consider them all as bad."[4]

You would not expect a five-year-old child to dabble in a blueprint for the construction of an airplane, and make it better. Evolutionists can supply no acceptable examples of improved kinds being created by mutation. When pressed, their most popular example is that of the Peppered Moth of Britain that temporarily changed proportions of light and dark colored moths related to the effects of the Industrial Revolution. This is, in fact, a clear example of *variation within kinds*, a product of genetic mixing created originally by God. It is like Darwin's finches and tortoises.

Woodpecker: Evolved?

Woodpeckers are quite valuable controlling those insects that attack trees, and they possess several extraordinary physical processes. Unlike other birds, their feet are anchored to the trunks of trees with two backward and two forward-facing toes, reinforced by sharp claws, and strong tendons and muscles, plus stiff tail feathers tipped with spikes.

These creatures eat as many as 2,000 ants, or hundreds of beetle larvae in a day. To locate them they peck fifteen or sixteen times a second, striking the tree trunk with one thousand times the force of gravity. To protect the bird's brain they are blessed with a much thicker skull than other birds, and the skull is separated from the beak by very effective shock-absorbing tissue. In addition, the beak is furnished with a chisel tip, and narrow nostrils protected from sawdust by tiny feathers.

Here is the part proving special intelligent design. To retrieve insects from the deep holes a one-of-a-kind, very long tongue is provided, beginning and anchored in the right nostril. It splits and passes beneath the skin over the right and left domes of the skull, and thence it passes into the floor of the mouth. To aid in retrieving insects this long tongue has bristles pointing backwards, and a special sticky glue to entrap the insects.[5]

Can you imagine how blind chance could possibly move the origin of the tongue from the floor of the mouth over the top of the skull to the right nostril?

[1] J.J. Friedn, *The Mystery of Heredity* (New York: John Day, 1971), pp. 315-316.

[2] C.P. Martin, "A Non-Geneticist Looks at Evolution," *American Scientist*, 41 (1953): 103.

[3] Theodosius Dobzhansky, *Heredity and the Nature of Man* (New York: Harcourt, Brace and World, 1964), p. 126.

[4] H.J. Muller in *Time, The Weekly Magazine* (11 November 1946), p. 96.

[5] David Juhasz, "The Incredible Woodpecker," *Creation ex nihilo*, Vol. 18, No. 1 (Dec. 1995–Feb. 1996), pp. 10-13.

Can you imagine how blind chance could possibly move the origin of the tongue from the floor of the mouth over the top of the skull to the right nostril?

64

REFLECTING ON LESSON NINE

1. What does DNA stand for? What does it do?

2. How many code words are represented in the DNA of simple bacteria? How many are represented in human DNA?

3. Can you explain how this DNA code might have developed? What is usually taught about it in the public schools? Knowing what you know now, does this seem reasonable?

4. What is a mutation? Are mutations usually beneficial or harmful?

5. Using the illustration of a child and a blueprint, what is the difference between a child and the designer who drew the plans? How does this apply to the random nature of mutations?

6. What do you think of the design of a woodpecker's head? How about the other specialized designs previously mentioned in this book?

10

T E N

BIOCHEMISTRY SLAYS THE DRAGON

A significant number of theologians have knuckled under to the beliefs of evolutionists, choosing to believe them rather than the eternal word of God. Unfortunately, evolutionary doctrine of creation is taught in many of the seminaries, and the preaching of the first two chapters of Genesis has practically disappeared. When have you heard a powerful sermon about creation? Yet, the four seraphim and the four and twenty elders are saying in Revelation 4:11 "Thou art worthy, O Lord, to receive glory and honor and power; [—why?—] for thou hast created all things, and for thy pleasure they are and were created." Many hymns and statements of faith become empty words without a belief in God as Creator.

Modern molecular biology has come to the rescue, and you can now cross your heart instead of your fingers. The sequence of amino acids in similar proteins such as hemoglobin in different animals can now be determined, and the differences in sequences can be compared.

An example of comparison is as follows:

(1) GDVEKGkKIFVMKCSNCHTV
(2) GDVEEGkLIEVMKCANDHTV

(Each capital letter stands for a particular amino acid. Differences are emphasized in larger type.)

In these two sequences there are five of twenty locations of amino acids which differ, representing a 25 percent difference. This numerical value of difference has been obtained and compared for bacteria, fungi, higher plants, cyclostomes, bony fish, amphibians, reptiles, insects, birds, and mammals. These differences have been carefully analyzed by Michael Denton, medical doctor, and biological scientist, who reports:

> **Yeast is as close to a human as it is to a monkey, pig, whale, tuna fish, or castor bean.**

> Each subclass is isolated and distinct. . . . No sequence or group of organisms can be designated as intermediate with respect to other groups. None can be recognized as being more primitive than another.[1]

> Despite these differences among groups, the astonishing observation is made that all eukaryotes (organisms which reproduce sexually . . .) are equally divergent from bacteria which reproduce by asexual cloning, and are considered by evolutionists to be the first organisms (prokaryotes). Thus, unicelled organisms such as yeast exhibit the same numerical sequence divergence from bacteria as does man, whale, fish, insect, or even higher plants. There is no suggestion in these sequence comparisons of any evolutionary pathway from bacteria, or any other groups of organisms. It is as though all proteins were carefully engineered with their own unique amino acid sequences.[2]

Michael Denton points out that when the protein sequence differences among subdivisions of the animal kingdom are analyzed, the same findings appear. Thus, among monkeys, gibbons, apes, and man, all are separate and distinct with no hint of transition from one species to another.[3]

Contrary to what one would expect if evolution were true, this data indicates:

A fruit fly is as close to a human as it is to a rattlesnake or an eel.

Yeast is as close to a human as it is to a monkey, pig, whale, tuna fish, or castor bean.

This very modern scientific technique shows that all forms of life are separate and distinct kinds. There is no evidence that any kind has changed into another kind. This modern, molecular science was not available to Darwin, but it proves what Austin H. Clark found after years of investigation of the relationships of various groups of animals to each other. "A backboned animal is always unmistakably a backboned animal, a starfish is always a starfish, and an insect is always an insect no matter whether we find it as a fossil or catch it alive at the present day."[4]

[1] Michael Denton, *Evolution: A Theory in Crisis* (Bethesda, MD: Adler and Adler, 1986), p. 279.

[2] Ibid.

[3] Ibid.

[4] Clark, *Zoogenesis*, p. 104.

[5] Behe, *Darwin's Black Box*, pp. 18-21.

Biochemical Vision

Michael J. Behe, associate professor of biochemistry at Lehigh University, has presented a biochemical sketch of the chemistry of sight.[5] The sketch is extremely technical, and I do not expect most of us to understand it, but I present a short résumé to acquaint us with the complexity and wonder of vision.

A photon of light strikes a retinal cell, and interacts with a molecule, 11-cis-retinal, which changes within a brief picosecond to trans-retinal. This binds to a protein, rhodopsin, which binds to another protein called transducin, which had already bonded with GDP. Several proteins and chemicals then interact and reduce the sodium ions in the retinal cell, which causes an electric current to be transmitted down the optic nerve to the brain, which interprets the vision.

The supply of 11-cis-retinal and sodium in the retinal cell would be depleted unless restored. This restoration is accomplished by a full paragraph of biochemical reactions.

The cycle is complete when trans-retinal becomes separated from rhodopsin by the action of several protein enzymes.

Darwin and millions of evolutionists have accepted the belief that the eye and vision could be formed and function by natural selection through unplanned, undirected chance. Now that we have this knowledge of how the eye works, there is no sense in believing that blind chance is our Creator.

REFLECTING ON LESSON TEN

1. Go back to the discussion of homology in an earlier lesson. If similarity did in fact prove close relationship, would we expect the similarities to be only in some areas or in all areas?

2. When we start comparing protein sequences, do they follow the same pattern of similarities and differences as outward appearance does?

3. Are the results of these biochemical comparisons surprising, or are they consistent with earlier scientific studies? In what ways?

4. What is presently being taught on the subject of origins in schools? Seminaries? Local churches? What should be taught?

11
E L E V E N

SEARCHING FOR UNCLE APE

Genesis 1:26: "And God said, Let us make man in our image, after our likeness; and let them have dominion over the fish of the sea, and over the fowl of the air, and over the cattle, and over all the earth, and over every creeping thing that creepeth upon the earth."

This prophecy was, and is, being fulfilled. Man is indeed master of everything that creepeth upon the earth. He is also made in the image of God, able to communicate with God, and able through the grace of Jesus Christ to have fellowship with God.

Alfred Russel Wallace, who independently formulated a theory of evolution and who joined Darwin in presenting the case for evolution to the Linnaean Society in London, disagreed with Darwin about the origin of man. Wallace was of the opinion that the human brain could not be explained through natural processes. Darwin did not include any scientific evidence to support his belief in *The Descent of Man*, and no evolutionist since Darwin has offered any rational scientific evidence for how the remarkable human brain might have evolved. The human brain consists of about ten thousand million nerve cells, and each nerve cell is in contact with other brain cells through ten to one hundred thousand connecting fibers. The total number of connections are estimated to be about a thousand million million. This is a number that is difficult to comprehend. It represents far more connections than all electrical connections in the entire world. How can anyone even imagine any random process producing such a treasure?

> Despite 137 years of searching, there are no fossils that have convincingly established man's descent from any other creature but man.

Evolutionary doctrine insists that man evolved from apes, despite the overwhelming evidence previously presented in this book. For some reason the press has been "apes" over the prospect for at least a hundred years. The press illustrators have drawn what they consider to be early man as brutish, hairy, and stooped. The concept has been responsible for the belief that some humans are inferior to others, with unfortunate results.

The search for "missing links" has continued since Darwin's time. *Despite 137 years of searching, there are no fossils that have convincingly established man's descent from any other creature but man.* Claims have been made, but all have been proven false. As Lord Solly Zuckerman, M.A., M.D., D.Sc. (Anatomy) has said: "As I have already implied, students of fossil primates have not been distinguished for caution when working within the logical constraints of their subject. The record is so astonishing that it is legitimate to ask whether much science is yet to be found in this field at all."[1]

NEANDERTHAL MAN

The first fossil claimed to be intermediate was so-called *Neanderthal Man*, found in the Neander Valley near Düsseldorf, Germany, in 1856. He was immediately pictured by the press as being bent, stupid looking, hairy, and ape-like — the prototype of "early" man ever since. His skull capacity and hence his brain was equal to or slightly larger than that of modern man. He was badly deformed in some ways, and the great pathologist of Vienna, Rudolf Virchow, after examination *declared him to be an old man with gout*. A fossil found in France in 1908 of an adult male was eventually discovered to have suffered from arthritis, the only reason he could not walk completely upright. Most of the Neanderthal people suffered from rickets, caused by lack of sufficient Vitamin D, producing deformities. Men of similar character have been found in France, and are called Cro-Magnon. Their cave paintings and artifacts show they were intelligent, sophisticated, and sensitive. If properly dressed they could walk our sidewalks and mingle with the crowds. Most anthropologists now classify the Neanderthals as fully human and the Cro-Magnon people as essentially identical to modern humans.

JAVA MAN

Eugene Dubois, a Dutch physician, determined, after Darwin, to find the "missing link" which he decided would be found in the Dutch East Indies. He was appointed a surgeon in the Royal Dutch Army in 1887 and sent to Sumatra. Sure enough, he discovered a piece of skull, three molar teeth, and a thigh bone on the Island of Java in 1891. He named his specimen *Pithecanthropus erectus* ("erect ape-man"), which he announced to the world as the "missing link." There followed much disagreement among paleontologists, but he was finally accepted as "Java Man" or *Homo erectus*. Typical of the "science" of paleontology, Dubois later admitted finding true human skulls in the rock formations not far from "Java Man," and still later he changed his own opinion and considered the skull cap that of a large ape or gibbon. Other expeditions to the same area have found only evidence of chimpanzees and gibbons.

An Austrian pathologist declared the first Neanderthal skeleton to be that of an old man with gout.

The finding of mixtures of human and other primate bones is not unusual, because primate brains are considered delicacies among many primitive people. The skulls are broken to obtain the brains, and various bone fragments of primates may be found among human artifacts and bones. The skulls of so-called "Peking Man," which were

72

allegedly found in caves of China, were probably of this origin. Like "Java Man," there are several unsatisfactory circumstances surrounding the claims of "Peking Man," and one of the most unusual is that the bones disappeared and have never been properly verified. Fully human bones were found in the same caves, and nothing but broken skulls of the primates were found. It would appear that men lived in the caves and ate the brains of poor orangutans.

> The findings of mixtures of human and other primate bones is not unusual.

PILTDOWN MAN

Piltdown Man was announced to the world with much fanfare in 1912, and given the scientific name *Eoanthropus dawsoni* ("Dawson's dawn-man"), having been discovered in a gravel pit near Piltdown, England by Charles Dawson, a lawyer and amateur paleontologist. He was proclaimed to be a "missing link" in textbooks and professional literature for over forty years.

In 1950 Piltdown Man was proved to be a fraud when he was finally submitted to scientific study. The skull was that of a human, and the jaw was that of a modern orangutan, whose teeth had been filed to appear human.

NEBRASKA MAN

In 1922 a single molar tooth was found by Harold Cook in Nebraska, and proclaimed to be that of a half-ape and half-man. It was given the scientific name *Hesperopithecus haroldcookii* ("Harold Cook's western ape"), and portrayed with his wife (!) in a portrait in the *Illustrated London News* as being an authentic ancestor of *Homo sapiens*. Evolutionists accepted him as "Nebraska Man," who lived 500,000 years ago. In 1927 Nebraska Man was shown to be nothing more than the tooth of an extinct pig.

These "missing links" strongly confirm the statement by Lord Solly Zuckerman which we quoted on p. 71.

AUSTRALOPITHECINES

Paleontologists continue to search for the elusive primate which they faithfully believe evolved into man. They are now enamored with the australopithecines. The first specimen, found in southern Africa in 1924, was named *australopithecus*, or southern ape.

The major living players in the game of seeking the hidden gorilla who might have fathered us all have probably been Donald Johanson and Richard E.F. Leakey, son of Louis and Mary Leakey.

In 1973 Johanson discovered in Ethiopia the knee joint of a small primate which he claimed to be outright an ancient hominid, intermediate between ape and man. The knee joint later proved to have no special significance regarding upright walking, but he eventually gathered about 40 percent of the skeleton which was of a female 3½ feet tall. He called his doll "Lucy," "human," "child," and "First Family," suggesting human status, wrote a book called *Lucy*,[2] and considerable sums of money and equipment became available. In the site where "Lucy" had been found a nearly complete skull was finally discovered which was clearly apelike.

Richard Leakey never attended college, had no special scientific education, and generally relied on others to evaluate his specimens. Leakey and Roger Lewin have also written a book titled *Origins* in which they unscientifically theorize: "The secret of human evolution is extreme adaptability, and the simple physical change that made this possible was the liberation of the hands from the basic function of locomotion."[3] So this was how the human brain was developed!

Most of the biology textbooks that are used to teach your children claim that humans evolved from apes. Where is their science? How DNA mutated to produce our brain is never described in textbooks, and DNA is never even mentioned once in Leakey's book.

Dr. Charles E. Oxnard, previous Professor of Anatomy at the University of

Paleontologists continue to search for the elusive primate which they faithfully believe evolved into man.

74

Southern California Medical School and Director of Graduate Studies, and now at the University of Western Australia, Perth, after multivariant studies of several anatomical regions of Australopithecus, concluded that they are uniquely different from both man and other extant primates.[4] Lord Solly Zuckerman, famous British anatomist, agrees with Dr. Oxnard's conclusions.

> You would hardly suspect the lack of evidence for ape-to-human evolution by reading contemporary writing.

Yet, you would hardly suspect this lack of evidence by reading contemporary writing, whether pop-up books for children or academic compilations. I can assure the reader the American Kennel Club would not certify an ancestor of your dog based on evidence such as paleontologists present.

---

[1] Lord Solly Zuckerman, *Beyond the Ivory Tower* (New York: Taplinger Publishing Company, 1970), p. 64.

[2] Donald Johanson and M.A. Edey, *Lucy, the Beginning of Mankind* (New York: Simon and Schuster, 1981).

[3] Richard E. Leakey and Roger Lewin, *Origins* (New York: E.P. Dutton, 1977), p. 38.

[4] C.E. Oxnard, *The Order of Man* (New Haven, CT: Yale Univeristy Press, 1984), p. 332.

Adam's Rib

Genesis 2:21,22 says, "And the Lord God caused a deep sleep to fall upon Adam, and he slept: and He took one of his ribs, and closed up the flesh instead thereof; and the rib, which the Lord God had taken from man, made He a woman, and brought her unto the man."

Centuries later, God must have told Moses, whom He had chosen to record the Pentateuch, about this first operation and anesthetic. Can't you imagine Moses complaining that people might question why men still have 24 ribs — and God telling Moses to go ahead and write it like He said? Lots of people have indeed questioned these verses.

We would not have an answer until thoracic surgery came to be. We now know that if we make an incision over a rib, split the periosteum (a fibrous covering of the rib), and remove the bony rib, leaving the periosteum in place, the rib will grow back! It is the only bone in the body that will grow back, and nobody but God would know that until maybe the late 19th century. The modern science of genetics also teaches that contrary to the early evolutionary belief of Darwin and Jean Baptiste de Lamarck, acquired characteristics are not passed on to offspring. We make big mistakes when we question God's word.

One of my daughters, Betsy Jernigan, pointed out to me the metaphor that Adam, like Jesus, was wounded to give life, and my wife, Peggy, added that Eve's life was bought by Adam's shedding blood, just as our life is bought by the shed blood of Jesus.

REFLECTING ON LESSON ELEVEN

1. Which of the suggested "missing links" fall into each of the following categories:
   a) Fully human?
   b) Ape?
   c) Intentional fraud?
   d) Completely mistaken identity?
   e) Transitional between ape and human?

2. Some people consider the heavy brow ridges on Neanderthal skulls evidence of "ape-like" features. Should we consider this characteristic any differently than the high cheekbones in some ethnic groups of the human race?

3. How much about the appearance of an individual can you tell from a skeleton? Can you judge amount or placement of hair? What does this tell us about artist's reconstructions?

4. Name ways that human bones and animal bones could get mixed up together in the same place.

5. How does Richard Leakey explain how apes developed into humans? Does this make sense to you? What academic qualifications does Leakey have to make such a statement?

12

T W E L V E

EXTINCTION FOR THE DRAGON

The book of Genesis establishes the very foundation of Christian doctrine, and God's authority. Jesus referred to these Scriptures for confirmation of many of His teachings. Those who seek to undermine Christianity attack the first few chapters of Genesis more than any others.

In this book the weakness of the theory of evolution has been shown. It is not science; it is belief, and it cannot be accommodated to the Word of God. As pointed out in Lessons 1 and 7, Darwin's selection of evolutionary examples are all really examples of variations within kinds, the products of God's creation of sexual reproduction. In Lesson 6 we learn that the origin of life from non-life is mathematically and biochemically impossible. In Lesson 8 the "experts" of evolutionary doctrine agree there is no proven example of a transition of one basic kind to another kind, and in Lesson 10 modern molecular biology has shown evidence that all forms of life are separate and distinct kinds, with no evidence that any kind has changed into another kind. Furthermore, evolutionists claim and teach that *the* method of change and increased complexity in organisms is by mutation. This is, indeed, surprising, because everybody should know, as shown clearly in Lesson 9, that mutations "never produce anything new,"[1] and that "all or almost all known mutations are unmistakably pathological . . . ."[2]

Finally, as explained in Lesson 4 there is overwhelming evidence that the earth is young — far too young to even entertain the theory of evolution, which demands millions of years.

I have already admitted that *I was led to accept parts of evolution by teachers who taught it as factually sound.* There are many who have been thus convinced. The theory is not a method used by God; it is an insidiously dangerous concept. It may well be the principle basis for the liberal theology of unbelief permeating the church. Josef Ton, who was pastor of the largest Baptist church in Romania, is quoted as stating: "Liberal theology is just evolution applied to the Bible and our faith."[3] He also quotes James and Marti Helfley, writing in *By Their Blood: Christian Martyrs of the 20th Century*: "New philosophies and theologies from the West also helped to erode Chinese confidence in Christianity. A new wave of so-called missionaries from main-line Protestant denominations came teaching evolution and a non-supernatural view of the Bible . . . the Chinese intelligentsia who had been schooled by orthodox evangelical missionaries were thus softened for the advent of Marxism. Evolution is destroying the church and society today, and Christians need to be awakened to that fact.[4]

Our public schools, universities, and most colleges are teaching evolution as fact, despite evidence such as I have submitted to you. Because the theory lacks substance, evolutionists bristle and resort to all manner of means to prevent the teaching of creation with evolution. So far their tactics are preventing your children from getting the facts, this despite a 1993 Gallup Poll which demonstrated that 47% of the American public believed humans were created by God about 10,000 years ago, 35% were theistic evolutionists, and only 11% believed the universe evolved naturally. In another poll 58% were for teaching creationism in public schools!

In much of our nation's history we enjoyed the blessings God promised in Deuteronomy 28:1-4a. "And it shall

> I was led to accept parts of evolution by teachers who taught it as factually sound.

come to pass, if thou shalt hearken diligently unto the voice of the Lord thy God, to observe and to do all His commandments . . . that the Lord thy God will set thee on high above all nations of the earth; and all these blessings shall come on thee, and overtake thee . . . . Blessed shalt thou be in the city, and blessed shalt thou be in the field. Blessed shall be the fruit of thy body, and the fruit of thy ground."

> Our children are being taught to despise God's word, to the destruction of our society's moral values.

Recently our great nation has begun following many of the nations, disbelieving God's word, and forsaking Him. We are beginning to suffer the consequences which He warned us about in Deuteronomy 28:15a, 16, 18, and 67. "But it shall come to pass, if thou wilt not hearken to the voice of the Lord your God . . . cursed shalt thou be in the city, and cursed shalt thou be in the field. Cursed shall be the fruit of thy body, and the fruit of thy land . . . . In the morning thou shalt say, Would God it were evening! and at evening thou shalt say, Would God it were morning! for the fear of thine heart wherewith thou shalt fear, and for the sight of thine eyes which thou shalt see."

Recognizing God's authority depends upon recognizing His Creation and believing His word. *Our children are being taught to despise God's word, to the destruction of our society's moral values.* We need to learn the facts, and become active in the decisions of our school boards, legislatures, and our churches. Instead of being taught that they are of no eternal value, our children need to *know* God's truth in Psalm 139:14. "I will praise thee; for I am fearfully and wonderfully made. Marvelous are thy works, and *that* my soul knoweth right well."

May the dragon evolution again suffer extinction.

Darwin's Spiritual Enigma

There have been conflicting accounts regarding Darwin's spiritual beliefs. We know his wife was a very devout Christian, and we know he studied for the ministry at Cambridge University, but chose not to be ordained.

For over fifty years claims have been made that he accepted Christianity toward the end of his life. One account which was circulated under the title "Darwin's Last Hours" quoted an English evangelist, "Lady Hope," as claiming that he asked her to speak to his servants and some neighbors about "Christ Jesus — and His Salvation." However, in a book edited by Emmett L. Williams, researched carefully, and written by Professor Wilbert H. Rusch and John W. Klotz[5] evidence is cited completely denying the authenticity of this report. In letters he characterized himself as an agnostic. It would appear that Darwin's spiritual belief was caught in the snare of his own theory, a continuing danger for those who accept the teachings of evolution as truth. He was chronically ill in his latter years with abdominal complaints suggestive of psychological distress, and as a doctor I am not surprised.

Shared Gifts

From Genesis we learn that pain and suffering were not God's original intent for us. Many agonize over the question of why we suffer if God claims to be loving and omnipotent and yet "allows" suffering. Scripture teaches us that original sin resulted in our suffering and death. Yet God has provided some wonderful healing mechanisms.

Our pain nerves are not all bad. Dr. Paul Brand,[6] retired master plastic surgeon and former missionary to the lepers of India, has taught how important pain sensation is to allow us to be able to perform routine acts such as walking, cooking, and handling rough objects without the necessity of forever consciously avoiding injury to our skin.

Dr. Brand has also taught that our spiritual demeanor influences our pain and suffering. Four states increase pain and four decrease. Fear and anger increase and peace and forgiveness diminish; idleness and loneliness increase while activity and visitation diminish. Healing mechanisms are also influenced spiritually. God has provided biochemical hormones including endorphins for pain relief, and also enkephalins to stimulate healing factors. Prayer has been scientifically proven to be a powerful influence for wellness. Happily, many of our previously totally secular medical schools are now teaching these healing modalities to medical students and practitioners.

All of us can benefit by recognizing and practicing these gifts of God.

[1] Dobzhansky, *Heredity*, p. 126.

[2] Martin, "Non-Geneticist," 103.

[3] Kenneth A. Ham, *The Lie: Evolution* (El Cajon, CA: Creation-Life Publishers, Master Books Division, 1987), p. 105.

[4] Ibid.

[5] Wilbert H. Rusch, Sr. and John W. Klotz, *Did Charles Darwin Become a Christian?* ed. by Emmett L. Williams (Flowery Branch, GA: Creation Research Society Books, 1988).

[6] Paul Brand, M.D., Lecture at Doctor's conference, Aqueduct Conference Center, Chapel Hill, NC, October 1982.

REFLECTING ON LESSON TWELVE

1. Is the theory of evolution truly scientific? Explain. What is the difference between science (which means "knowledge") and belief?

2. Did Darwin and evolutionists since Darwin describe evidences of evolution or variation within kinds?

3. Does mutation appear to be a satisfactory method of developing new kinds of organisms?

4. What can believers in biblical creation do about what is being taught in schools without running into problems with the so-called "separation of church and state"? Is it fair to expect schools to make the kinds of decisions we want unless we get personally involved?

5. What has God promised to nations which pay attention to and abide by His teachings? What future can we expect if we ignore what He tells us?

6. How does disbelief in God contribute to acceptance of evolution? How does belief in evolution lead to rejection of God? What can we do about this two-sided problem?

7. Do you believe the earth is closer to 6,000–10,000 years old, or 4.5 billion years old?

FOR FURTHER READING

Biology

Behe, Michael J. *Darwin's Black Box*. New York: The Free Press, 1996.

Cooper, Bill, B.A. (Hons.). *After The Flood*. Chichester, West Sussex, England: New Wine Press, 1995.

Darwin, Charles. *The Origin of Species by Means of Natural Selection*. New York: A.L. Burt Co., 1909.

Denton, Michael. *Evolution: A Theory in Crisis*. Bethesda, MD: Adler & Adler, 1986.

Gish, Duane T. *Evolution: the Fossils STILL Say NO!* El Cajon, CA: Institute for Creation Research, 1995.

Johnson, Phillip E. *Darwin on Trial*. Washington: Regnery Gateway, 1991.

Manly, Isaac V., M.D. *God Made*. Joplin, MO: College Press, 1994 and 1995.

Morris, Henry M. *Creation and the Modern Christian*. El Cajon, CA: Master Book Publishers, 1983.

Sunderland, Luther D. *Darwin's Enigma*. Santee, CA: Master Book Publishers, 1984.

Wysong, R.L. *The Creation-Evolution Controversy*. Midland, MI: Inquiry Press, 1976.

Geology

Brown, Walt. *In The Beginning: Compelling Evidence for Creation and the Flood*. Phoenix, AZ: Center for Scientific Creation, 1995.

Morris, John D., Ph.D. *The Young Earth*. Colorado Springs: Creation-Life Publishers, Master Books Division, 1994.

Whitcomb, John C. and Henry M. Morris. *The Genesis Flood*. Phillipsburg, NJ: Presbyterian and Reformed, 1961.

Education

Gish, Duane T., Ph.D. *Teaching Creation Science in Public Schools*. El Cajon, CA: Institute for Creation Research, 1995.

Ham, Kenneth A. *The Lie: Evolution*. El Cajon, CA: Creation-Life Publishers, Master Books Division, 1987.

For more information on Creation-Science issues:

Center for Scientific Creation
5612 North 20th Place
Phoenix, AZ 85016

Creation-Life Publishers, Inc.
P.O. Box 26060
Colorado Springs, CO 80917

Institute for Creation Research
P.O. Box 2667
El Cajon, CA 92021

ACKNOWLEDGMENTS

I am daily conscious of my wife Peggy's great faith and witness for our Lord Jesus Christ, and grateful for her encouragement. My whole family including Kathie Bell, Betsy Jernigan, Peggy Graddy, and son Sawyer Manly have supported my efforts, and patiently listened to my discourses.

John Hunter, editor of College Press Publishing Company, suggested this relatively short version of my previous work, *God Made*. I am grateful for his sage advice and encouragement.

Three scientists whom I greatly respect were gracious to evaluate my manuscript. They checked my science, and even my punctuation, and provided valuable advice, for which I am thankful. They are Dr. Gerald Van Dyke, Professor of Botany and Plant Pathology at North Carolina State University, Raleigh, North Carolina; Michael Kinnaird, Ph.D. in Organic Chemistry, Director of Research and Development for a specialty chemical manufacturing firm, and President of the Triangle Association for Scientific Creationism; and Charles Liebert, a member of Ken Ham's Creation ministry, *Answers in Genesis*, and teacher of both children and adults in classes and seminars.

Duane T. Gish, Ph.D., Senior Vice President of Institute for Creation Research, and prolific author and lecturer for creationism was also kind enough to review and make valuable suggestions for this material. I humbly give thanks to God for all who have helped.

Most of all I have treasured God's guidance. He has supplied my needs, and I pray that the Holy Spirit will use this material to strengthen your understanding of Jesus Christ's love and the knowledge of His Creation, His Kingdom, and His authority.

Amen